What people are saying about

Writing Worship

"I have had the privilege of watching Krissy walk out this book through life and cowrites for years now. I am inspired by her talent but more so by her heart for the Lord and for equipping other people. In this book she is giving away knowledge that would take someone twenty-plus years to gain through writing songs every day! No matter what stage or skill level you are at when it comes to songwriting, you will take away a deeper knowledge of not only practical songwriting techniques but also what really matters when it comes to writing songs for the church. This book is a must-read for anyone wanting more of Jesus and more songs!"

Mike Grayson, worship experience director at Cross
Point Church in Nashville, staff writer at Centricity
Music, and former lead singer of MIKESCHAIR

"I am so excited that this wonderful book will finally be in the hands of many who ache to bring new songs to the table … songs that glorify God and give expression to 'kingdom come on earth.' Krissy Nordhoff is one of the generals in this realm—a true craftsman of songs, a true worshipper of God, a true lover of people, and a true believer in helping others. I know that if you carefully and prayerfully apply the principles she shares in *Writing Worship*, the songs will come, whether for an audience of the One or many. Allow Krissy's heart and wisdom to lead you to the table, where everyone is welcome, and I believe that through the gift of love and time, you will find yourself deep in the art of writing before you know it."

Darlene Zschech, songwriter ("Shout to the Lord"),
worship leader, author, and senior pastor of HopeUC

"Krissy carries the heart of the Father and the kingdom of God with unspeakable depth. This isn't just any book—this is an awakening of identity and destiny. You're about to go to a whole new level!"

Jenni McGrew, founder of Worship Leaders
Collective and influencer of worship leaders

"Very few people have encouraged me in songwriting like Krissy has. She is a gifted songwriter who has devoted her life to helping others find their voice. This book should be read by anyone who wants to write songs for the church. It is not just for the professional, but it is for anyone who has ever dreamed of writing a song. As Krissy will tell you, "Everyone is invited to the table.""

Dustin Smith, artist and songwriter

"I have written songs with Krissy, and she doesn't just write songs—she becomes the song! Her focus and passion on saying just the right words with just the right melody is her trademark, along with keeping the process fun and heartfelt. You will learn so much from reading Krissy's book, *Writing Worship*, and will be inspired to write your new songs immediately. Dive in! Take the journey into the world of songwriting with Krissy."

Paul Baloche, Dove Award–winning singer-songwriter
and founder of LeadWorship

Writing Worship

Krissy Nordhoff

Writing Worship

How to Craft Heartfelt Songs for the Church

DAVID C COOK

transforming lives together

WRITING WORSHIP
Published by David C Cook
4050 Lee Vance Drive
Colorado Springs, CO 80918 U.S.A.

Integrity Music Limited, a Division of David C Cook
Brighton, East Sussex BN1 2RE, England

The graphic circle C logo is a registered trademark of David C Cook.

Library of Congress Control Number 2019948101
ISBN 978-0-8307-8079-2
eISBN 978-0-8307-8080-8

The Team: Michael Covington, Alice Crider, Rachael
Stevenson, Kayla Fenstermaker, Susan Murdock
Cover Design: Jon Middel
Cover Photo: Getty Images

Printed in the United States of America
First Edition 2020

1 2 3 4 5 6 7 8 9 10

121819

I dedicate this book to aspiring worship songwriters.
I hope you hear my heart for you through these pages,
cheering you on with deep sincerity. Never forget
that no matter what opposition you face, your voice
is valued by the King and needed by the church.

Contents

Acknowledgments

Thank you, Mom and Dad, for being such a steady love and support my entire life and for planting in me the love of Christian music. To my siblings, Patti, Maribeth, and Buddy; my grandparents; and my extended family; thanks for all the times you came to hear me sing.

Mike and Ulrike Nordhoff, thank you for caring so well for us over the years.

Thank you, Steph, Cherie, Donna, Dawn, Deanna, Lisa, Jacquie, Laurie, Angela, Stacey, Carole, Jill, Andrew, Hector, Dustin, Harry, Scott, and Lydia for holding me up when I needed it most.

Thank you, Ray, for telling me who I am.

Thank you, Wisdom, for your guidance.

Brave Worship, you are the reason I know the beauty of true community. Thank you.

Worship Songwriter Mentorship small-group leaders, Amanda, Emily, Lani, and Rachael, thank you for carrying the message and awakening songs in others so beautifully.

To my cowriters, not only my songs but also my life is so much better because of you.

To the artists who have carried my songs, thank you for partnering with me to build the kingdom in ways I never could have on my own.

To Integrity Music and my tribe at David C Cook, thank you for believing in me, showing me the path, and walking beside me.

To Eric, my husband, thank you not only for encouraging me to follow my dreams but also for partnering with me every step of the way (especially with technology!). We make a good team, and I love you. When you write your book, I'll edit it.

To my children, Alex, Kaden, and Anthem. I never want you to feel that you have to follow in my footsteps when it comes to music. I only pray you follow my heart. There is plenty of it here in this book, and I hope this is part of the legacy that will last past your generation. I love you and all those coming after you.

Jesus, You already know. But thank You for being the bread I need every day.

Introduction

Join Me at the Table

Worship songwriting. That one phrase has the potential to stir up many thoughts and feelings. If you have never written a song, it may bring up dreams and anticipation. If you have explored songwriting a little, it may cause you to want to learn more. You might simply love worship, and the idea introduces a new avenue of expression. Maybe your songs have already had an impact in some way and this phrase stirs up greater possibility. But you could also have a lot of questions or have even experienced rejection in this area, so worship songwriting incites fear.

At one time or another, I have experienced all these thoughts and emotions. I want you to know, no matter what you are feeling as you step into this journey, this will be a safe place for you. A safe place to explore, learn, make mistakes, and grow.

With all that is in me, I know that song is meant to be an integral part of our faith. There is a connection between head and heart that is ignited only through song. It's meant to be woven through our everyday, our gatherings, our joys, our sorrows, our prayers. And if songs are meant to be so common, then maybe those who write them should be too.

The table of the Lord is vast, stretching much farther than we can see. All are invited to this table. Just when we think it's getting full, our Carpenter, with His own hands, will expand it. It never ends. He just keeps telling us to gather more chairs.

Do you simply want to observe how songwriting works? There's a chair for you. Are you ready to get your feet wet? There's a chair for you. Do you want to analyze and understand? There's a chair for you. Would you like to spend time with Jesus in a new way? There's a chair for you. Do you want to learn more about the skill of songwriting? There's a chair for you. Have you felt crushed by someone, but you still can't shake your dream? Let go of the past and come sit by me.

There will be many conversations at our table. It's only fitting that I introduce myself to you and share my story. I'll share my journey from dreams to Doves and everything in between so you can have a glimpse of the ups and downs, the joys and frustrations, of a songwriter's life. Then we will answer the question this whole book hinges on: "Why do we need new songs?" This will be the foundation for everything we do moving forward.

Once we move past the small talk, we'll dive deep into the heart. We'll talk about what's different in worship songs than in other songs. You'll learn that they have to be birthed from the intersection of honesty, love, discipline, and sacrifice. We'll discuss how to stay in a place of real worship—not just for songwriting but for your relationship with the Lord—through reading God's words and two-way journaling. There are many obstacles, which I call boulders, that can get in the way of worship, and I'll show you how to clear them.

Along the way you will have time to process what you learn and listen for what God has to say to you personally.

But heart is not all we'll explore. I will also introduce many tools and teach new skills, starting with the Songwriter Personality Test. This test will tell you what kind of songwriter you are, your strengths and weaknesses, and what kind of writers would be a good match for you in a cowriting situation. I'll share with you what helped me learn more about worship songwriting than anything else—singing and analyzing the Psalms. We'll delve into mapping songs and discover how to give them great structure and support while keeping everything on target. We'll study what the verses, chorus, and bridge need to say. We'll hear about some practical tools for our songwriting, as well as common pitfalls to be aware of. I'll pinpoint some resources that you should have at your fingertips as you write.

We'll cover all things cowriting: how to find a cowriter, the three ways of cowriting, how to get started, and some tips that will help along the way. As we go, you'll put each aspect into practice one at a time (including the cowriting!). All these tools eventually combine into one long Song Critique Checklist, which you will use to learn the skill of critiquing your own songs and why that is important.

As we wrap it all up, I will share about the song that has been in my family's blood for centuries. I will also tell you about my favorite song, Anthem, and how God determined her life and course, just as He does all songs. The purposes for all these songs may be much larger than you realize, and I will expound on what all those may be.

And then, the blessings. I will pray for you and send you off with the Songwriter's Commission.

Before we go any further, though, I want to be sure we are fully prepared. These are a few recommended supplies:

A journal. This will be helpful, especially for your two-way journaling sessions. You may like to use it as well for psalming (singing the Psalms aloud), song-mapping brainstorming sessions, and just plain songwriting.

Your favorite Bible. You will need a Bible translation handy as we explore psalming and read God's words. If you need a suggestion, I really love the creativity of *The Message* and *The Passion Translation.*

Your favorite musical instrument (optional). Playing an instrument is great but not necessary! Keep yours close by if you play one, as there will be plenty of opportunities to incorporate it.

Internet access. A laptop, tablet, or smartphone will be helpful. I will mention several websites and online resources you'll want to be able to reference.

Speaking of online resources, I want you to know that there are many additional resources online for this book, including printables, videos, and audio recordings. It's my hope that these additional resources will greatly enhance your experience with the book. Take advantage of them! I will direct you to them one at a time, but feel free to explore them anytime along the way at www.krissynordhoff.com/book.

To squeeze every bit of goodness out of this book, I highly recommend doing all the suggested exercises. There is a method to all this; everything we do is intentional. It will all fit together by the end, and you'll understand it in much greater ways if you do not skip these steps.

Through our time together, I hope to equip you, nourish you, and invest in you, the carrier of worship yet to be. I pray that reading

God's words, two-way journaling, and psalming become daily practices that seep into your heart and your music. My desire is for you to discover a lot more about who you were created to be and how you fit into God's family. I also pray that all the skills and tools you'll learn are exactly what you need to begin and continue crafting songs for your local church. You have a great purpose, and I want you to see that. The kingdom needs *you*.

Oh, and one more thing. There is no need for perfection here. Just be completely you. Mistakes are OK. I'm pretty sure our cups will be running over and there will be lots of feasting. Things could get messy. But isn't that exactly what a family table looks like?

So will you join me? I've been praying for you. And I've saved you a seat.

1

Songwriting Is a Journey

*Only those who will risk going too far can possibly
find out just how far one can go.*

T. S. Eliot, preface to *Transit of Venus: Poems* by Harry Crosby

For me, writing songs began somewhere between the butterfly-spotted hills of my family farm in southwest Michigan and my grandmother's organ. Somewhere between hymns and "El Shaddai."[1] Without understanding or even thinking, I simply sang what rose to the top of my heart. Many times I stood on the crossbar at the end of my metal swing set in the backyard and sang into the pole that ran across the top because it echoed like a microphone.

My first music teacher was my grandma Millie. She played the organ and the piano by ear and completely captivated me. She was the first to move my little fingers onto the right keys to plunk out the melody to "Heart and Soul." Grandma Millie went to heaven when I was almost five years old. My young heart was broken. But years later, I realized that was the same year my first official song floated into the air near the back pasture of that farm. Now I understand that this mantle of music was an inheritance.

Through childhood my love of songwriting continued to grow. Without realizing it, I became a student of lyric and melody. I used to play a game whenever a new contemporary Christian music album came out. I would listen to the record bit by bit and write down all the lyrics as they came (repositioning the needle or rewinding the cassette as needed). I would then compare them with the official lyric sheet to see how many I got right. (Only a lyricist would think this was fun!)

In our little country church, I would study the hymnal, noticing depth and themes and rhyme and patterns, sometimes for the whole service. It was there I learned the hymn "Take My Life, and Let It Be," which contains these lines: "Take my voice, and let me sing / Always, only, for my King."[2] They took root in me for good when I was fourteen.

As I got older, I traveled with my family, singing "special music" in different area churches. Dad brought my little sound system (bought by my grandma Josie), along with my background tracks, and functioned as my tech team. Mom took me to piano and voice lessons during the week and cleaned the teacher's house in exchange for my lessons since we couldn't afford to pay her. Their support was sacrificial. They always believed in me.

My first recording was in high school. I sang in a Youth for Christ choir, and they chose to feature one of my original songs on their album. Soon after, I was able to attend Anderson University by the grace of God in the form of a scholarship. It was there I took Songwriting 101 from Gloria Gaither. I left that class with tears many times because of how deeply I was moved by God's heart through her teaching. I would've attended all four years just for that class. I didn't know then how much my life would be affected by it, but I know now.

I saved the final requirement for my degree, an internship in the music business, for last. I knew the Lord was calling me to move to Nashville, and I wanted to do the internship there. The week before I was to move, I had no job, car, apartment, health insurance, or internship. Still, I knew I had to go. Within a week, all those things fell into place in a God-orchestrated way I couldn't understand.

Soon after moving to Nashville, I was offered a record deal. We negotiated it all with the lawyers, and I was assigned a producer to work with. When they gave me the tour schedule, I saw that I would be gone for two to three months at a time. I was ready. But about six months into those negotiations, the company decided to drop me. I felt devastated.

Around that time I met my husband, Eric. He had already been working in the Christian music industry for several years, directing international sales for Warner Alliance, Provident, and Word. Eric had the business experience I didn't and was able to help me navigate those waters.

The closer we got to marriage, the more I began to question God's will for my life. I really wanted to have a family. It felt like the first priority in my heart. I began to question if I would be OK traveling for two to three months and leaving my family at home. When I got really honest with myself, the answer was no.

I made the decision to be an independent artist, writing and singing all my own songs. It gave me the flexibility with family that I wanted. It ended up working out well since family quickly followed marriage! We had been married a year and a half when Alex, our oldest, was born. Within twenty-three months, Kaden was born. These two little boys won my heart, and I was so thankful. I wrote songs during little windows like nap time and after I put them to bed. They were good travelers and came with us as I did concerts from Texas to Michigan and everywhere in between. I added some time for the kids in many Sunday services. And they "helped" me sell CDs. It was a sweet time. One Sunday we did two services in the morning, then drove four hours to do a festival that night, boys in tow. After that day I began to feel a season shift. I knew something needed to change.

The next week I found out I was expecting our third child, our daughter, Anthem. It was during that pregnancy that I cowrote "Your Great Name"[3] with my home church in mind.

Ultimately it was recorded for our church album. It was the song that taught me to let go. I had never written a song that I didn't sing. The night we performed the song for the first time, I was in the choir and very pregnant! I heard the Lord tell me, "Sing in the choir this time and watch what happens." Soon the entire congregation was on their feet.

As the song's popularity began to grow and Natalie Grant chose to record it on her album, I realized something for the first time: I could write songs and stay home with my kids, and my songs could travel. It had always been an option, a possibility, but I had never seen it.

So I began to settle into this "I'm a songwriter" identity. However, if I'm honest, I have to say I feared I had missed something for years.

Until one day when the Lord whispered to me, "I can use you in much greater ways if you will write songs for Me."

Another time, I was driving to Nashville to record a song story video with my cowriters. We would be asked to share about how the song was inspired, how the song took shape, and what it meant to us. I couldn't even remember the song, so I pulled it up on my phone to listen and tried to remember the details before I got there. I heard the studio singer belting out the melody I had crafted, and I thought, *Oh yeah, that sounds like me. I can hear my inflections there.*

Then I heard God's voice say, "Do you know what I hear when I hear your songs?"

I replied, "No."

He answered, "*Your* voice. I hear *your* voice."

I burst into tears, thinking about how many times He heard me. That is all that mattered. "Take my voice, and let me sing / Always, only, for my King."

I had known, ever since those lyrics settled in my heart, that I would be involved in Christian music. But in the early days of my writing, worship as we know it wasn't yet a thing in church culture. I started out writing simple songs about Jesus. But in college that changed to more clever, wordy songs. Then I wrote plenty of songs just to process my own emotions—even songs to release anger (ask me about "Alcatraz"[4]). I wrote about my experiences as a mother, a wife, a daughter. I wrote songs to teach my kids lessons and values I didn't want them to forget.

Then came worship. I didn't understand it at first. In fact, it was pointed out to me that the songs I was recording and singing were not congregational worship because I used the first-person (I) viewpoint.

It didn't make sense to me that using first-person pronouns could make such a difference. It felt like worship to me. Learning what it meant to write congregational worship took a while.

Some people say Nashville is a seven-year town (meaning it takes seven years to have a breakthrough in your music), but it took fourteen years for me to get my first cut (one of my songs recorded by an artist). I was in town for nineteen years before signing a publishing deal. Most recently I've been a staff songwriter for Integrity Music. Some of my songs have been sung by artists and worship leaders such as Mandisa, Darlene Zschech, Tauren Wells, David and Nicole Binion, and Natalie Grant. I have loved serving both artists and church worship teams as I've helped them write songs for their records and congregations. I'm so thankful.

While I have so much to be grateful for, this journey hasn't always been an easy one. As soon as I got to Nashville, I could tell it was going to be interesting learning to navigate industry, family, and ministry. I began to pray for a mentor. I asked the Lord if He would connect me with a woman who had walked these places before I had, someone who could shepherd me through some of the questions and situations I faced.

I repeatedly encountered the "Nashville No," which is basically when people show support or make promises to you face to face but later won't answer your phone calls or texts (it's a cultural way of saying no or that they are actually not interested). One time I encountered an industry woman who heard my songs and then laughingly called herself the Dream Crusher. I have had cowriting sessions canceled and faced many other challenges simply because I'm female. At one point someone said to me, "Thirty is old in the music business. If you were twenty-five, I would sign you to a record deal today." I almost gave up after that one. Funny enough, I saw no breakthroughs with my music until after I was thirty-five.

I continued to pray for a mentor for fifteen years with no answer. Finally that fifteenth year, the Lord said, "Be what you need." That's when I stopped looking to get something and realized just maybe I had something to give.

I chose to start pouring into the generation behind me, and I have been mentoring songwriters for ten years now. I noticed that songwriters needed community, so I started Girls Write Out, a gathering for female writers. That eventually became a ministry called Brave Worship, which I cofounded with my sister Maribeth Dodd, who is a worship leader. You can check it out at braveworship.com. Through that ministry I saw a need for more hands-on songwriting instruction for women as well as men. That was the beginning of the Writing Worship Course and the Worship Songwriter Mentorship (for more about these, see pages 167 and 168). Then I saw a need for a book in which I would go into more detail. And that, my friend, is what you now hold in your hands.

I know these twenty-five years of writing in Nashville—the trials, the mistakes, and the joys—were not for me alone. They were also for you. I've thought about you in writing rooms, at writers' nights, at church, and as I've prayed. I know your journey as a songwriter will be unique, but I also know there are insights I can share with you that will encourage and equip you in all the ways I once so desperately needed. All I know I freely and joyfully give you!

Let's begin with why the church needs *you* to write new songs.

2

The Need for New

Let us sing a new song not with our lips but with our lives.

Saint Augustine

In the music industry we're seeing a cultural shift toward writing original worship. More and more worship teams are traveling to Nashville to learn how to craft songs, and I spend many of my days working with them. Recently I sat down to write with some worship team members from Life.Church, Craig Groeschel's church. They told me their goal is to write 70 percent of their own worship songs within the next year. They aren't the only church moving this direction.

It seems like a new phenomenon, but in fact it is a very ancient practice. For centuries, people groups have created their own songs, their own sounds. It was only in the 1970s that Nashville and the music industry became the gatekeepers of church music. Part of that was simply because of the available methods of distribution. Music began to funnel through record labels and was distributed by them as well. With the internet, though, distribution and marketing have changed again. Now there is a marketing platform accessible to everyone. Churches are forming their own publishing companies as well as writing, recording, and releasing their own songs. These songs are landing on Christian music charts like Billboard.

More songs are available to the church now than ever before. Do we really *need* more? And why should we write original songs for our churches instead of simply singing songs that are popular in the church at large? Before we go any further, let's answer these questions. I see five significant reasons that new worship songs have been and will continue to be needed by the church.

New Songs Bring Fresh Praise and Fresh Revelation

God loves fresh praise. Yes, we have praised Him before. But in any relationship, it takes creativity and intentionality to continue growth. How many times have you told the same person you love him or her? God will never tire of fresh praise because it means love and depth. It blesses Him every time.

The Bible contains many references to singing, and there is a clear emphasis on the *new song* and how it praises His name. Psalm 96:1–2 says, "Sing to the LORD a new song; sing to the LORD, all the earth. Sing to the LORD, praise his name; proclaim his salvation day after day" (NIV).

I absolutely love that God tucked the command "Sing to the LORD a new song" several times into the Psalms, the oldest worship songs, because He knew we would have them for a long time. That way, if we got stuck on the old ones, we would have to be reminded to sing new ones. Even the book of Revelation mentions new songs around the throne (see 5:9; 14:3)! The new song of praise is meant to be eternal.

Sometimes the newness in our praise happens through lyric. Sometimes the newness in our praise happens through melody or sound. Sometimes it's a different form or structure. Sometimes it's spontaneous. But it's always fresh.

Have you heard the song "Surrounded (Fight My Battles)"[1]? That song was birthed out of a live worship set. It's totally different from most songs out there today, but it's fresh. I love the bold newness in that song.

Just as the Lord loves fresh praise, we love fresh revelation. Have you ever sung a new song that expressed how you had been feeling for a long time and suddenly you had words to articulate your emotions? Have you ever felt like your eyes have been opened to understand a truth, which you may have already known, in a much deeper way? Have you ever seen Scripture begin to connect in new ways? Has God given you fresh insight about your purpose? That's revelation! Revelation always fills us back up with hope and peace.

John Calvin spoke about this revelation, saying, "Till the Lord opens them, the eyes of our heart are blind. Till the Spirit has become our instructor, all that we know is folly and ignorance. Till the Spirit of God has made it known to us by a secret revelation, the knowledge of our Divine calling exceeds the capacity of our own minds."[2]

When we are born again, "the Holy Spirit opens our eyes so that we can see who God is and who we are for the very first time," and after we are saved, "He continues to work to give us insight into His revealed Word and to deepen our personal relationship with Him."[3]

We all have the opportunity to receive insight like this firsthand by spending time with Jesus. He promises that when we seek Him, we will find Him (see Jer. 29:13). New songs are a way to express these new revelations from Him to us and to the church. I regularly pray that my songs will be not simply bearers of information but deliverers of revelation! There's a big difference.

New Songs Speak a Dialect

I grew up in Michigan, so I have a midwestern accent. My son once asked me if I was from another country, and I replied, "Pretty much." That was even after I'd lived in Tennessee for many years. Once, while shopping in the clothing section at a Target store in Tennessee, I approached the fitting rooms to try a few things on, and an elderly woman behind the counter asked me a few questions. Her voice sounded so familiar to me, though I had never met her. I asked her where she was from. She said, "Allegan, Michigan." My hometown. I couldn't believe I could hear that specific accent.

While describing the day of Pentecost, the Bible says, "When they heard this sound, a crowd came together in bewilderment, because each one heard their own language being spoken" (Acts 2:6 NIV). That chapter goes on to record Peter's message to the crowd and says that three thousand people came to believe that day (see v. 41). There was such an amazing harvest because they could hear what was being said in a way that spoke to them personally. Jesus has a way of doing that—of finding ways to speak to us individually. I believe He has the same desire for congregations when it comes to worship songs.

Did you know your church has its own dialect? A mother tongue. I know because I've written with many church leaders as they've come through town. As we talk and begin to get to know each other before cowriting, I can hear it in their conversation. If I ask more questions, I discover phrases the pastor says a lot. Words that are off limits. Different denominational beliefs. A powerful message from the pastor that has become part of a congregation's vocabulary. I'm telling you, if you write in your church's own dialect, your songs have such a personal approach to worship that lives will change because the message is more specific and sounds like home.

I've seen many online debates about certain worship songs. Sometimes lines are rewritten (rewriting any copywritten lyric always requires permission from the publisher). Songs can be written for any church dialect. Maybe your church needs someone to rise up and write them.

New Worship Songs Bring Unity to the Church

A church that has the ability to write original worship songs has a unique opportunity to bring unity to the church staff. Having conversations and seeking the Lord about certain topics are great ways to grow together. Questions such as "What is the Lord speaking to you this week?" and "What Scripture are you studying right now?" may seem simple but can become amazing Holy Spirit connections for the team. It's awesome when the pastor is willing to engage in these conversations with the worship leaders and songwriters in the church.

These conversations will bring unity not only to the staff but ultimately to the entire church. This is because the songs written will emphasize and accelerate the message the pastor is preaching. When you put a message to melody, you help everyone remember the teaching well beyond Sunday morning.

I've been writing a lot with the worship staff at Cross Point Church in Nashville. The pastor, Kevin Queen, has been speaking about waiting on the Lord, so we wrote a song about that. It's breathtaking when they sing it!

I've also seen unity develop the opposite way. Recently Pastor Queen heard a new song we had written for the church based on a quote from one of the members who has ALS (aka Lou Gehrig's disease). He was so inspired that he scrapped the message he was supposed to preach the next Sunday and rewrote his whole sermon around the new song. It was one of the most powerful church services I've ever experienced.

New Worship Songs Minister to the Congregation

Whether in times of challenge or victory, worship leaders and songwriters have an opportunity to meet the congregation right where they are.

Worship songs help us gently approach people experiencing trials and lead hearts to healing. Often we can encourage through song as we never could through the spoken word. We get to remind people going through hard things that God loves them and will never leave them no matter what.

Songs can also help us celebrate a victory like a sea-crossing moment. I love the story of the Israelites crossing the Red Sea. After they arrived on the other side, Miriam pulled out her tambourine to worship the Lord with a new song (see Ex. 15:20–21). If your church has experienced a breakthrough that only the Lord could have orchestrated, you need to celebrate! Maybe five hundred people just got baptized. Maybe there's a new building. Praise the Lord with a new song!

Sometimes God will speak the same theme to many individuals in a congregation at the same time. This happened at my church not too long ago. I wrote a song called "Back to Life." It was birthed out of my daughter walking through extreme anxiety. The bridge says this: "Resentment, depression and all anxieties, / They have no power over me. / Addictions and strongholds and every disease, / They have no power over me."[4] We had some reservations about those words in the writing room and how they would go over in a worship set. But the first Sunday we sang that song with our congregation, people began recording it on their phones. Several people asked me after the service where they could get the depression song. They were all dealing with it! The Lord used that song to minister to them as He ministered to my family at the same time.

God can also use songs to minister to a congregation outside the official worship time. Sometimes this looks like one song shared one friend at a time. Maybe you write a song for a friend who's grieving. Maybe you write a song for a family celebrating an adoption. These songs are a great way to bring encouragement or celebration in a more intimate way by affecting individual members of a congregation. I believe this has a bigger impact on the congregation and kingdom as a whole than we realize.

Whatever the circumstance that birthed them, songs can minister to people in all situations!

New Worship Songs Prepare Congregations for the Future

I was recently studying about prophets in the Bible, and I was amazed to find that many of them were also songwriters. Some of the greatest prophets in the church may very well be part of our worship teams.

"Watch What He Will Do" is another song I wrote with Cross Point Church. It's a call for revival. The bridge goes like this:

> *You better get ready for a miracle*
> *You better get ready for the joy*
> *You better get ready for revival*
> *'Cause it's coming; it's coming*[5]

This is the heartbeat of where the church is feeling called to go but has not yet been. Putting this message on their lips now will prepare them for where the pastor feels they are being led: revival.

I once brought a song to my congregation called "Fighting for Us."[6] One of our most precious members was battling cancer during that time. Tears streamed down her face as she worshipped the Lord with complete abandon. We didn't know that a few months later she would be in heaven, sitting at the feet of Jesus. Since her passing, when we sing it with her family in the congregation, I realize

"Fighting for Us" means something different now. Only God could have known the full purpose of why we wrote that song.

So, yes, new worship songs bring fresh praise and fresh revelation, they speak a dialect, they bring unity to the church staff and congregation, they minister to the church, and they prepare us for what's ahead.

Do I think original worship songs are all we need? Absolutely not! In the Bible, Paul mentioned "psalms and hymns and spiritual songs" (Eph. 5:19 KJV). Psalms, as we know, were the old songs. It is believed that hymns may have been instructional songs. And spiritual songs ... well, those could have been spontaneous or new songs.[7]

Any way we honor Him with song is beautiful, but this passage reminds us we need balance. Oftentimes, when we get out of balance, it's because we are missing the new songs. Not on my watch!

3

Worship Songs Begin in the Heart

Let God have you, and let God love you—and don't be surprised if your heart begins to hear music you've never heard and your feet learn to dance as never before.

Max Lucado, *Just Like Jesus*

Worship songs are different from any other songs we could write. Styles and trends in music are always coming and going. Uses of sounds and instruments too. What was popular even five years ago in the world of worship is completely different now. For instance, I was told not to use first-person pronouns like *I* and *me* in worship songs before, but now many worship songs include them. I never would've thought I would be able to address the topic of addiction in a worship song, but I now have a song that does exactly that. In the past, most worship songs had close to an octave range, but now we are seeing that expand some. And whereas we have seen a lot of spontaneity recently in worship songs, I believe we will see a circling back toward liturgical worship next. Honestly, a lot of these shifts have to do with what is speaking to our culture or churches. Just as new songs keep things fresh, so do the new stylistic elements.

But none of these things—production, instrumentation, style—define what a worship song is. Those elements are the vehicle that delivers the song. The heart of the song is hidden inside. The heart of worship never changes.

There is one thing that completely sets worship songs apart, which will always be true of any of them: the focus of the song is Jesus, God, and the Holy Spirit, not us. Any other type of song has a different theme; hip-hop, country, dance, folk, even opera—they all focus on people or objects. But when a worship song plays, we remember how much Jesus matters.

Psalm 95:6 says, "Come, let us bow down in worship, let us kneel before the LORD our Maker" (NIV). Humble hearts focused on Him. As long as that happens, it's worship.

However, many worship songs have some basic characteristics. These characteristics are good guidelines to follow for modern worship. Not all of them will be in one song, but all worship songs have some of these traits.

I could've called these the Ten Commandments of Worship Songs, but I didn't! Viewing them like the laws from the Old Testament that God gave to Moses is actually not a bad idea. The laws were given ultimately for our good. But then grace broke through. The same will be true here. These characteristics are meant to remind us of some great markers, but there is grace.

We do have to keep the focus on God, Jesus, and the Holy Spirit, or we are no longer writing a worship song. We also need to maintain biblical accuracy. Nearly everything else is negotiable.

Top Ten Characteristics of Worship Songs

1. A worship song should be true and biblically accurate because song teaches theology. (Example: "In Christ Alone"[1])

2. Worship songs have community voice. Many times a worship song uses *we* pronouns. For instance, "We are all here worshipping You." (Example: "Holy Spirit"[2])

3. Simple, memorable melody and lyrics are important. You want people to be able to sing and worship more than they have to think. (Example: "Good, Good Father"[3])

4. Staying close to an octave in range helps. Yes, some singers can jump the octave, but giving an option for the congregation to sing is key. (Example: "Ever Be"[4])

5. Worship songs often contain elements already familiar to the church. Incorporating part of a hymn into a new song is one way to do this. (Example: "Amazing Grace [My Chains Are Gone]"[5])

6. Hope is always present thematically. A worship song never ends in a sad place. Even in the hard times, we know redemption is coming. (Example: "Blessed Be Your Name"[6])

7. Worship songs show a greater picture. They take us out of our microscopic perspectives and show us the world at large in Jesus. (Example: "How Great Is Our God"[7])

8. A worship song can tell the story of the gospel. (Example: "How Deep the Father's Love"[8])

9. Worship songs call us to respond, whether it's raising hands, dancing, or even running into His arms. (Example: "Forever Reign"[9])

10. A worship song can remind us of what's to come! (Example: "Revelation Song"[10])

You already understand why we need new worship songs, and now you have a clearer picture of what's contained in great worship songs. Before you dive into the writing, though, you need to remember where it all truly begins: your heart.

The Birthplace of Worship Songs

You may assume that worship songs are birthed in the very room in which they are written. The moments when the song structure takes shape. The emerging of a lyrical hook into the atmosphere. The marriage of word and melody. But when I dissect these songs, trace their genealogy, I see that most of the time they began way before then. Worship songs begin in the heart.

Sometimes we get the idea that writing worship requires some sort of perfection of the heart. Actually that could not be further from the truth. But worship does require honesty. The most authentic worship songs originate in the intersection of honesty, love, discipline, and sacrifice.

Honesty

The hour is coming, and is now here, when the true worshipers
will worship the Father in spirit and truth, for the Father is
seeking such people to worship him. God is spirit, and those
who worship him must worship in spirit and truth.

John 4:23–24 ESV

Whenever I sit down to write with people, I always ask how they are doing. This one question opens the heart's doors. So many things spill out. Struggles, joys, fears—all of it. If someone is going through marriage issues, we talk about it. If someone is dealing with unbelief, we remind that person of the promises.

My friend Cheryl recently said at the beginning of a writing session, "Guys, I can't write a worship song today without telling you … even though I've hardly told anyone yet … but I have to be honest before we can write. I'm pregnant!" Real, raw life. I always make room for these things before we worship or write. Sometimes I will stop and pray right there. Why? Well, I love people, and I have the gift of mercy. But I also know if we are not worshipping Him from an honest place, it's not going to be true worship! Your honesty is a filter that worship runs through. Never let this filter get stopped up.

Love

I love you, LORD; you are my strength.

Psalm 18:1 NLT

This song is a beautiful example of David expressing true love. His heart overflowed after this statement, naming God his rock, fortress, deliverer, shield, horn of salvation, stronghold, and more. David said His way is perfect and the word of the Lord is flawless (see v. 30 NIV). Sounds like love to me! He went on and on describing all the ways the Lord had worked in his life. He was worshipping from the overflow.

Sometimes when I'm writing, I'm overwhelmed with love for the Lord too. Most writing days, I ask if we can start with worship. Ninety-nine percent of the time, a worship song is birthed from this free-flow worship time. Out of pure love. As with every aspect of worship, this love will run through the honesty filter; it has to be real.

Discipline

Worship should be a well-worn path.

Darlene Zschech

It took me years to learn to appreciate the beauty of discipline. But I have found that when I take time with the Lord in the morning, I hear Him much louder in my cowriting sessions. The same voice that speaks to me when I'm by myself speaks to me in the writing room. But I had to learn His voice in the quiet place first.

Reading the Word, praying, and journaling are part of my everyday. That's how I continue to grow in my relationship with the Lord. We have conversations; there's revelation. Sometimes I get so excited about what the Lord reveals to me that I can't wait to get into the writing room. Sometimes I leave that time with questions. Sometimes it's crickets. Every day is different. But over time there is more growth and more depth. Eugene Peterson called it "a long obedience in the same direction."[11] Some days I feel like getting up. Some days I don't. But I do. I've seen too much fruit. I've had too many life-changing encounters.

The same is true of writing in general. I call most of my writing buried treasure. These are songs you really have to dig for. They take hard work—strength and perseverance. Some of my buried treasure took years to finish. But the beauty about the practice of buried-treasure songs is that if you are faithful with them, your skills will be sharp and you will be well prepared should a gem simply fall from heaven. Those are the kinds of songs that seem to be dropped from the sky and require ready hands to catch.

Through the art of discipline, worship becomes a reflex.

Sacrifice

I will not sacrifice to the LORD my God burnt
offerings that cost me nothing.

2 Samuel 24:24 NIV

When we walk into worship—whether alone with the Lord, in a cowriting situation, or in a worship-leading situation—and we expect to *get* something, we've got it wrong. Seeking platform, success, or visibility under the umbrella of worship won't work. (Remember the honesty filter.) In fact, we should be worshipping only for the sake of giving. And many times the giving costs us something. It may cost a little; it may cost a lot. Hebrews 13:15 says, "Through Jesus, therefore, let us continually offer to God a sacrifice of praise—the fruit of lips that openly profess his name" (NIV). True worship is a sacrifice. As stated in 2 Samuel 24:24, David refused to offer to the Lord a sacrifice that was free.

Smith Wigglesworth once said, "Great faith is the product of great fights. Great testimonies are the outcome of great tests. Great triumphs can only come out of great trials."[12]

And I would add, great songs can come with a great cost.

Read stories of "It Is Well with My Soul,"[13] "Amazing Grace,"[14] and "I Can Only Imagine"[15] and you will see the cost I'm talking about. I want you to remember, though, that God will never require more sacrifice than He gives blessing (see 2 Cor. 4:17–18).

On many occasions I've walked into a cowriting session only to hear someone say, "I want to write a song like 'Your Great Name.'" I understand what those people mean to some degree. But I also want to say, "Do you know what you're asking for?"

The Story of "Your Great Name"

In 2002 I was diagnosed with advanced-stage Lyme disease. Honestly, the diagnosis was a relief. I had been to so many doctors, some of whom thought my problems were mental. But this one believed me; he knew because his wife had nearly died of Lyme disease. He explained to me the long road ahead. There was a long list of oral antibiotics, other medications, and supplements I would need to take. Since each antibiotic would kill only one form of the bacteria and it had the ability to morph into three forms, we would have to try combinations and frequent changing of antibiotics to have the best chance of eradicating it. The supplements were needed to try to keep my gut healthy despite the number of antibiotics I was going to take. The timeline would depend on how my body handled the detoxification process. I had to change my diet drastically and continue exercising. I got started immediately.

I remembered a tick bite during my first pregnancy. I remember getting so sick the next day and going to my doctor immediately. He told me that if I didn't get a rash, it couldn't be Lyme disease. I wish that had been true. Throughout that pregnancy and the next, I experienced a lot of fatigue, twitching in my back, knee pain, and sudden blood-pressure issues. It was all chalked up to pregnancy.

I endured three and a half years of these symptoms before I was told I had advanced-stage Lyme disease. By that time I had experienced joint pain throughout my body, felt twitching and tingling all over, had a hard time walking, had severe migraines daily, and even struggled to sign my name. I remember praying that I would be able to make dinner for my family and do one load of laundry per day. That was all the strength I had. My husband was traveling a lot, doing international sales for Christian music, and I was home with our two small boys. I had lots of time to press into the Lord.

One night I was in so much pain that I got up, lay facedown on my living room floor, and planted my face over my Bible. I asked the Lord to speak to me. Not in an "I have to search for hours" kind of way. He knew I needed Him immediately. I cracked open my Bible to John 11:4: "When Jesus got the message, he said, 'This sickness is not fatal. It will become an occasion to show God's glory by glorifying God's Son.'"

I was glad to read that, because I thought I was dying. I took that verse as a promise of redemption and healing.

After my diagnosis I continued antibiotics for eighteen months. We reached an ending point in the doctor's eyes, and he decided to take me off. He warned me that most people get worse after going off the medication, and if that was the case with me, I would need to start IV antibiotics. That seemed impossible considering my two- and four-year-old boys.

Right about that time, my sister Patti called me from Michigan, telling me about a healing service her church was doing. She invited me to come. I prayed about it and felt as if God was saying He would meet me there. I was pretty nervous about it all, as I had never seen prayer for healing in the church I grew up in. But I knew I had to go. When the pastor prayed for me, I felt an electric love touch my body. I heard the Lord say to me, "And that was just My fingertip." Given my Reformed and Wesleyan upbringing, I didn't really understand what had happened, yet something had. (I've since attended Church of God [Anderson], Foursquare, Baptist, Church of God [Cleveland], and nondenominational churches. I'm a spiritual mutt. There's something beautiful in every one.)

I knew everything had changed in that moment. He was healing me not only physically but also spiritually and emotionally. I couldn't believe He loved me so much. That healing was for me. It rocked my faith, who I was, how I prayed, and how I wrote songs. Everything.

Within two months, all my blood work was clear.

Soon afterward a little boy in my home church in Tennessee got sick. I remember asking to pray. Even asking to start a healing ministry. My heart was so on fire and full of faith. I did get to pray for him. He had a terminal illness, and it was literally all that could be done. For the first time ever, our church held a service specifically to pray for healing for this little boy. And within one week, he went home to be with the Lord.

Everyone in the church felt crushed. I saw fear set in among us about praying for healing. It was understandable.

But something welled up in me. I knew the Bible said to pray for the sick (see James 5:14–16). And God heals every time, whether it is here or there. I didn't want to stop praying.

I had been studying the Psalms and happened to be on Psalm 136 during this time. I loved the repetition of "His love never quits."

All these things swirled in my heart as I sat down at the piano, wanting only to proclaim the *truth* about who the Bible says God is, no matter what life looks like. And I began to sing these words:

Lost are saved, find their way
At the sound of Your great name
All condemned feel no shame
At the sound of Your great name
Every fear has no place
At the sound of Your great name[16]

So it began. This song went through several stages and a couple of writing sessions that took my core concept in various directions. I couldn't feel settled about where it was landing. I didn't want to give up on it. Michael Neale, my worship pastor at the time and cowriter, knew all too well these sentiments I had experienced. He had walked the journey with the family of the sick boy too. He understood.

Michael's discernment confirmed my sense that the song wasn't quite there yet. I went back to the original core concept and invited him in to see if he could help me write the full song that needed to be sung. He took my verses home and returned with the chorus and bridge. He said, "We've been talking about the power of His name in the verses. I think the chorus should start with His name … Jesus." Together we put the final touches on every section, sending ideas back and forth via email. After these revisions, we agreed it was complete.

The price of that song was Lyme disease. It cost me two years in bed, having barely enough energy to take care of the basics for my family. It was paid for in tears on the way home from the park with the boys because my knees wouldn't work. I lost my ability to sign my name at the doctor's office. So many migraines and sleepless nights. And I had to walk through a family's sorrow over their son. That's not to mention what the song may have cost Michael.

But the blessings. Oh, the blessings. I experienced healing in fullness, and I will never forget. I started to understand the love of the Father for the first time. I began to see that I mattered to Him. I gained great mercy for the sick and passion to pray more fervently. My faith grew exponentially. My husband and children got to watch the process of healing happen before their eyes. I began to eat cleaner. I began to exercise more. My spiritual well got deeper. The joys seemed sweeter. My songwriting bloomed.

And then God redeemed in an unexpected way. He took this song and blew His Spirit on it. It was recorded. It became a radio single. It was nominated for and won a Dove Award. Testimony after testimony poured in. I remember seeing one that said, "I got saved to this song." Even now it makes me tear up. Some said that song got them through a hard time. Some said they were so thankful to hear my story of Lyme disease, because they had it too. Some said it was their favorite song. Their life song.

God took the sacrifice and turned it into a gateway of blessing. I say that with fear and trembling. I still can't believe what He did.

The roads you walk will be different from the roads I walk. Whether small or large, sacrifice is nothing to be afraid of. It's *always* worth it.

"Your Great Name" was not written primarily at my piano. It was born from gut-wrenching, honest pleas in the middle of the night that were answered with healing revelation about who Jesus is. It was given breath on the floor of a church, where I knew He loved me and I loved Him back. It emerged from the discipline of pressing into Jesus and His promises when I didn't know if I still believed I would see them come to life. It arose from the sacrifices of pain I never wanted to make and from seeing the most amazing blessings as a result. It's the most authentic place I've ever been. Is it a perfect place? No, it's messy, that crossroads of worship: honesty, love, discipline, and sacrifice. But it's real. And I never want to be anywhere else.

4

Staying in the Crossroads

The printed word is a thought you can see.
Bobby Conner

How do we get to the crossroads of worship? And how do we stay there? It simply comes down to being with God. "Seek first the kingdom of God and his righteousness, and all these things will be added to you" (Matt. 6:33 ESV).

There's a big difference between knowing about God and knowing God. I began to know God when I began to study His words for myself. I grew in my understanding of who He is as provider, redeemer, healer, rescuer, and so much more. I began to see all the prophecies in the Old Testament fulfilled in the New, and they showed me God's faithfulness. I saw time and time again how He was true to His promises. I saw promises for me. I learned many basics of how to live in a God-pleasing way—basics about everything from finances to conflict. I learned how powerful God is, how creative He is. I read stories of people being delivered through trials, and I was so encouraged with hope that He could deliver me from my trials too. And He spoke to me.

Reading God's words is hearing God speak. It's moving, challenging, inspiring. It's foundational to faith. It's necessary for relationship.

But it's important not only to your faith. If we are going to write lyrics that bring hope to the church, then we'd better know God's words. There is nothing more powerful and life giving to sing than the truth of His words. Writing is a great responsibility, and songs are teachers of theology. As Pastor Charlie Weir once said, "Songs are sticky. They'd better be true."

You may be reading God's words already. You may have your favorite translation and a read-through-the-Bible-in-a-year calendar. You may need some help with where to start (the New Testament is a good place). That's OK too.

I have read different translations over the years: the King James Version, the New International Version, and the New Living Translation. I love changing things up because it gives new perspective and understanding. Recently I have loved the *The Message* as well as *The Passion Translation*. For the creative, they are so poetic.

Now, I know we can get legalistic with these things, but that's not what I'm saying to do. I remember a busy exam week in college when I was just checking the box on my daily Bible reading and the Lord showed me this verse: "Come with me by yourselves to a quiet place and get some rest" (Mark 6:31 NIV). The Lord understands seasons too. There have been times I prayed a prayer of thanks for having thirty seconds to wash my hands by myself when I had three littles. He knows, and there is mercy.

The best advice anyone has ever given me on reading the Bible was given by Pastor Harry Stambaugh. He charged me with reading daily, starting with five minutes each day. Five minutes sounded doable, even in my busiest life seasons. What started as short and easy grew to much more. Not because I had to, not because I was checking a box, but because all the pressure was off and I fell in love.

I want to pass on that challenge to you. If you're not already reading daily, try starting with five minutes. You won't believe what you can learn in a short amount of time. See if you can stop at five!

Two-Way Journaling and Prayer

Nothing can make you desperate to hear Jesus like trials. I believe He's speaking all the time, but we stop to listen more often during a trial. Between 2014 and 2018 I was desperate to hear. My dear friend Laurie walked with me through those days. She began sharing with me about a new way she was hearing from the Lord, a concept called two-way journaling. Laurie invited me to a class where it was used to hear God speak. I went, having no idea I was about to find the other half of my prayer life.

Two-way journaling is writing out scriptures, prayers, questions, feelings. And then … it's waiting and listening for an answer. I had never given Him room to speak to me like this. He actually will! Listening for God this way can help songwriters like you and me greatly. We hear fresh new things, which God loves to continue to reveal to us when we give Him room. Not only do we grow in our relationship with Him, but we fill our creative tanks at the same time.

A word of caution, however: two-way journaling and prayer without being in the Word of God and in community can be a dangerous place. You could be hearing your own thoughts and thinking it's Him. Share your thoughts with those you trust, and make sure everything lines up with Scripture. Those two things are vital.

But it's beautiful! I've never experienced Jesus as I have through two-way journaling. He has encouraged me, told me what's to come, and given me so much wisdom and strength. I've learned how much prayer is a two-way conversation!

I then began to discover that this template, this conversational approach to communicating with God, is in the Bible. I had never seen it before. But it's true. Look at David's conversation here with the Lord. This very well could be a two-way journaling entry!

> Keep me safe, O mighty God.
> I run for dear life to you, my safe place.
> So I said to the Lord God,
> "You are my Maker, my Mediator, and my Master.
> Any good thing you find in me has come from you."
> *And he said to me*, "My holy lovers are wonderful,
> my majestic ones, my glorious ones,
> fulfilling all my desires."
> Yet there are those who yield to their weakness,
> and they will have troubles and sorrows unending.
> I never gather with such ones,
> nor give them honor in any way.
> Lord, I have chosen you alone as my inheritance.

You are my prize, my pleasure, and my portion.
I leave my destiny *and its timing* in your hands.
Your pleasant path leads me to pleasant places.
I'm overwhelmed by the privileges
that come with following you,
for you have given me the best!
The way you counsel and correct me makes me
praise you more,
for your whispers in the night give me wisdom,
showing me what to do next. (Ps. 16:1–7 TPT)

I couldn't believe it. It was right before my eyes all along, and somehow I'd missed it, this two-way conversation.

So my journaling began. Day after day I practiced the discipline of reading God's words, praying through my pen, and listening. I was fed over and over with revelation that amazed me. I want to share with you a few of my journal entries so you can see how varied they can be. There is no right or wrong method here; simply let the Holy Spirit guide you.

A Simple Conversation

Me: Lord, I saw a hammock yesterday, and someone was praying in it! Just like the one I prayed in.

Him: If I showed you only big, impressive revelations, you would revere me as God. But when I show you these intricate details, give you joy in a million little coincidences, you know me as Father. Fathers know details of their children's hearts. They notice what brings them joy and love to surprise them with it.

A Bible Passage Broken Down

"When Jesus saw her condition, he called her over and gently laid his hands on her. Then he said, 'Dear woman, you are free. I release you forever from this crippling spirit.' Instantly she stood straight and tall and overflowed with glorious praise to God!" (Luke 13:12–13 TPT).

He said,

- "Dear woman"—a precious address, showing compassion.
- "You are free"—a statement of truth, prophetic upon hearing but immediately actualized! He is speaking exactly opposite of how she has been feeling and operating the last eighteen years.
- "I release you"—He has the power to bring freedom, and He is giving it now.
- "Forever"—sometimes demons come back and bring more with them, but He is freeing her forever.
- "From this crippling spirit"—whoa. Crippledness can be a demonic spirit. He didn't tell her body to be healed, realigned, and restored. It already was. It was simply suppressed. He released the demon, and her health was visible!

I wonder how many times this woman prayed for healing, when all the while she just needed a prayer of freedom.

An Analogy

I stood before my nearly empty pantry and thought, *It looks like all ingredients!* As in nothing I could eat immediately. I heard You whisper to my heart, "That's what I give you. Ingredients. Prayer, worship, Bible, journaling, etc. It's up to you to put them together with time and effort to get fresh bread."

I have all the ingredients I need!

Word Trails

I have used the e-Sword app on many occasions while journaling. This is also something I learned in my journaling class. I love this app because you can research the meanings of words in their original language. You can also find other places a word occurs in the Word of God. Sometimes tracing a single word will lead me down a beautiful path of revelation. Here's one example of a word trail.

My songwriter friend Joshua Silverberg told me last week that bread is healing for children. Sure enough, Matthew 15 talks about it. Verses 24–28 say,

> He answered, "I was sent only to the lost sheep of Israel."
>
> The woman came and knelt before him. "Lord, help me!" she said.
>
> He replied, "It is not right to take the children's bread and toss it to the dogs."
>
> "Yes it is, Lord," she said. "Even the dogs eat the crumbs that fall from their master's table."
>
> Then Jesus said to her, "Woman, you have great faith! Your request is granted." And her daughter was healed at that moment. (NIV)

Bread = Healing

Matthew 7:9 says, "Which of you, if your son asks for bread, will give him a stone?" (NIV).

The word translated "stone" is *lithos*, which can be paired with other Greek words to mean "a millstone" or "a stumbling stone," something to take someone down. (Here begins the trail.)

I realized the same word, *stone*, appears in Matthew 28:2: "Behold, there was a great earthquake: for the angel of the Lord descended from heaven, and came and rolled back the stone from the door, and sat upon it" (KJV).

The resurrection was a triumph over stone. Over the heavy things that make us stumble and fall, the opposite of healing! Now the stone has been rolled away, and Jesus gives us daily bread—daily healing. Thank You, Lord!

Matthew 4:3 states, "Then the tempter came to entice him to provide food by doing a miracle. So he said to Jesus, 'How can you possibly be the Son of God and go hungry? Just order these stones to be turned into loaves of bread'" (TPT). This verse references stumbling being turned into healing. But that was not the way Jesus would turn stone to bread; rather, it was through the cross and the literal stone of the tomb being rolled away!

Do you see a pattern here? Yes, I love researching the topic of bread. It all started with a two-way journaling session with the Lord.

The Vision of Bread

God, do You have fresh manna for me today?

I see You baking fresh bread, and it smells so good. I see You pulling it out of the oven with a large wooden paddle. I see the bread. On the bread is written *intimacy*. I'm supposed to eat it. It tastes amazing, but somehow I've been gluten free this whole time. What have I been missing? Whoa. I've been spiritually gluten free for years, picking and choosing which bread I will eat. Afraid of some, thinking it will hurt me. Maybe afraid of intimacy too. Oh, Jesus, help me daily eat the bread You put in front of me. I'm sorry, Lord. I've been afraid to eat, and all the while the bread was called intimacy. Help me eat what You put in front of me. I don't want to be a picky eater.

Be it trials or triumph, there is goodness in the bread. It will feed me what I need. Keep my heart hungry. Oh, Bread of Life, be as irresistible to me as a fresh-baked loaf. Let me never skip the manna You have for me each morning. There is something about the morning, isn't there, Lord? It's the time You chose to give the manna. And I also know that manna didn't last more than one day. Yes, Lord, I see it now. No one can live on stale, moldy bread. It's the fresh bread that gives life. I need it every day. Help me remember that skipping meals or eating junk other than Your goodness will leave me spiritually malnourished.

This was a life-changing moment for me. I immediately went out that day and bought fresh wheat berries and made bread. I had to smell it. I had communion with my husband. I never would have guessed that there were so many layers of meaning in something so simple. God spoke through pictures, and then He spoke through smell.

For several months after seeing this vision, I awoke to the smell of fresh bread around five o'clock in the morning. I believe this was the first time God has spoken to me through the sense of smell. I'm not one to keep sleeping when I smell food! So it totally worked. I believe it was a reminder of the fresh bread He had waiting for me in the morning. I was so drawn in. This continued for a few months. Sometimes at the first scent I felt so tired still. Then I remembered … it's gonna be *so good*! One day I even woke to the smell of burnt toast. I got up and looked all over my house to see who had been up making toast at five o'clock. No one! I heard the Lord say to me, "That's what you're gonna get if you don't get up early! Your bread will be burnt toast!" Ha ha! Finally my body clock was set to the right time, and I stopped smelling the bread. But I've never stopped craving the fresh bread of His presence.

John 6:33–35 says, "'The true bread of God is the one who comes down from heaven and gives life to the world.' 'Sir,' they said, 'give us that bread every day.' Jesus replied, 'I am the bread of life. Whoever comes to me will never be hungry again. Whoever believes in me will never be thirsty'" (NLT).

This verse came to life for me because of the experience I had with the Lord about bread. I see bread everywhere now … in the Lord's prayer (see Matt. 6:11), in Jesus' parable about yeast (see Matt. 13:33), in the feeding of the five thousand (see Matt. 14:13–21). This has been a recurring theme in my walk with Jesus. Many times the revelation He shares with me comes to mind in the writing room. Out of this bread journaling, for instance, I wrote a song called "You Are the Bread."[1]

Songs help me remember these revelations.

Friend, I pray the same breakthroughs, revelation, and deepened relationship with Jesus for you through two-way journaling. He promised that if we seek Him, we will find Him (see Matt. 7:7 NIV).

I've been teaching my ten-year-old daughter about two-way journaling and prayer, and it's been amazing. In her first entry, she asked God, "How are You?" She heard Him answer, "I am great!" When I told her His name is the *great I AM*, she was so excited.

It doesn't have to be complicated to be meaningful. In fact, most of the time it's so simple.

Spending time with the Lord this way will greatly help you remain at the crossroads of honesty, love, discipline, and sacrifice. I'm going to give you some ideas that will help as you get started. Then, as we finish this chapter, give it a try. Start with five minutes.

Tips for Getting Started

- For us creatives, background music can be distracting, so I recommend either silence or something like white noise or a rain sound playing quietly.
- Read your Bible before you start. Knowing God's words will help you discern when it is Him speaking and when it is not. Also, when you finish journaling, make sure what you heard lines up with Scripture.
- Consider downloading the e-Sword app for help with biblical research.
- Give yourself grace for the process. Remember, it may take a while to experience a life-changing journaling session.
- Share your journaling with a trusted friend who's a believer, and ask for feedback.
- Be patient. My daughter once asked me if I had ears in my heart, because she thought I could hear God and she couldn't.

I reassured her that we are born with one set of ears, but the other set grows as we practice.

Ideas for What to Write About

- Research a word or phrase on e-Sword that stood out to you during your Bible reading. Journal about it and ask God what He has to say about it.
- Ask God a question such as "God, do You have fresh manna for me today?"
- Tell God where your heart is and how you are feeling, and ask for a response.
- Write out a prayer. Spill your heart on paper. Listen for His heart to respond.

Suggestions for When You Get Stuck

- If you are having trouble hearing Him and He wakes you up during the night, get up! I have found that is the easiest time to hear, when nothing will distract. Psalm 17:3 says, "In a visitation of the night you inspected my heart and refined my soul in fire" (TPT).
- Try typing your journaling on a computer. Some songwriters have found words flow much easier that way.
- Change your setting. Go someplace else, like a coffee shop or a library. "Change of pace + Change of place = Change of perspective."[2]

Two-Way Journaling Time

Let's do it!

- Take some time now to read God's words.
- Next, begin to journal. You may already know what you'd like to talk to the Lord about, or you can use one of the ideas from the previous page. Pour out your thoughts; then listen for His voice and write down what He says.
- Continue journaling as a daily practice as you work through this book and beyond.

If you work two-way journaling into your daily practice of gathering bread, along with reading God's words, your heart will stay in the right place—the center of the crossroads of honesty, love, discipline, and sacrifice. Keeping your heart in this place is essential for your life and for your songs. True worship songs ooze these characteristics. Nobody can connect with contrived or fake worship; it's gotta be the real deal.

As we move forward, we will build on what we've learned in this chapter. We will do more two-way journaling exercises in this book, and you can visit www.krissynordhoff.com/book to see more examples of two-way journaling.

The more bread you eat, the fuller you and your songs will be. Keep reading God's words; keep journaling! Stay centered.

5

Clearing Boulders

Create in me a pure heart, O God, and renew a steadfast
spirit within me. Do not cast me from your presence or take
your Holy Spirit from me. Restore to me the joy of your
salvation and grant me a willing spirit, to sustain me.

Psalm 51:10–12 NIV

Now that you've had a taste of two-way journaling and you know
where the four roads intersect, let's talk about possible roadblocks.
The enemy will try to shut down those roads of honesty, love, discipline, and sacrifice. Especially in the lives of those who have great
potential to serve the church and further the kingdom of God, like
worship songwriters.

There are many ways he tries to shut us down: unforgiveness,
pride, depression, anxiety, self-hatred, addiction, guilt, shame, anger,
judgment, fear, pressure, unrest, doubt, negativity, stress, people
pleasing, self-pity, busyness, overserving, workaholism, the need to
control, lies about who we are, selfishness, distraction, fatigue, and
illness, to name a few.

The enemy will throw these things right in the middle of our roads, where they serve as boulders that trip us up, slow us down, even stop us from getting to the center of that crossroads.

Sometimes the enemy will tempt us to make choices with our flesh until we give in (sin). More boulders. Sometimes we agree with him more than we agree with the Lord. More boulders.

I used to believe there would be one day when I would sort of arrive spiritually or at least get closer to a level of perfection. The process was so frustrating to me. But the longer I walk with Jesus, the more I realize the point of our relationship with Him is not arriving, because that is self-sufficiency. We are created to need Him continuously.

Don't be surprised; just keep working on clearing your road. You know the boulder breaker. He can clear the way. He can make your path straight (see Prov. 3:6 NIV). His plan is always redemption.

How does this happen? First we need to identify which boulders are in the way. Which obstacles are tripping you up, slowing you down, or stopping you?

Identifying Boulders

Grab your journal; then ask Jesus to help you with these questions, referencing the boulders mentioned above:

1. Is there anything blocking me from being honest?
2. What is keeping me or distracting me from loving You?
3. Is anything keeping me from the discipline of spending time with You?
4. Who or what is stopping me from sacrificing?

At times we may have a lot of boulders. Remember, the Lord is gentle in the way He leads us. He has compassion on us and is so kind. Most of the time that means we work on one thing at a time, although that is not always the case. He could clear them all at once in a supernatural second. Be patient with the way He leads you; it will be different from how He leads anyone else.

When the boulders are on the periphery, we can find ways around them and become accustomed to them. I encourage you not to modify your steps according to the boulders. Move the boulders so you have more freedom for your steps!

Hopefully your journaling has helped you identify the first boulder that needs to be cleared. Identifying a boulder is half the battle!

Next, we need to think about the part we had in creating this boulder. Maybe it's unforgiveness blocking the road of honesty. Maybe it's busyness blocking the road of discipline. In any case, we are going to take a moment to go before the Lord sincerely and *confess* and *repent*.

1. Take a moment to ask the Lord this question: Lord, how have I contributed to _____ being a boulder in my life? See what the Lord has to say in response. Let your heart be open to what He has to say; He only wants to heal you. Listen now with your pen.

2. First John 1:9 says, "If we confess our sins, he is faithful and just and will forgive us our sins and purify us from all unrighteousness" (NIV). I urge you to, with this promise in mind, knowing He *will* forgive, to journal your confession and repentance to the Lord now. Then listen with your pen.

Be assured, when we identify boulders, admit where we were wrong, and ask for forgiveness, Jesus hears. He not only hears; He also forgives and clears the boulders!

My favorite songwriter of all time is King David. Look at this psalm with me. In it David was going through the very process we are talking about—confession and forgiveness that ends with a song.

How happy and fulfilled are those
whose rebellion has been forgiven,
those whose sins are covered *by blood*.
How blessed and relieved are those
who have confessed their corruption to God!
For he wipes their slates clean
and removes hypocrisy from their hearts.
Before I confessed my sins, I kept it all inside;
my dishonesty devastated my inner life,
causing my life to be filled with frustration,
irrepressible anguish, and misery.
The pain never let up, for your hand of conviction
was heavy on my heart.
My strength was sapped, my inner life dried up
like a spiritual drought within my soul.
  Pause in his presence
Then I finally admitted to you all my sins,
refusing to hide them any longer.
I said, "My life-giving God,
I will openly acknowledge my evil actions."

And you forgave me!
All at once the guilt of my sin washed away
and all my pain disappeared!
　Pause in his presence
This is what I've learned through it all:
All believers should confess their sins to God;
do it every time God has uncovered you
in the time of exposing.
For if you do this, when sudden storms of life
　　　　overwhelm,
you'll be kept safe.
Lord, you are my secret hiding place,
protecting me from these troubles,
surrounding me with songs of gladness!
Your joyous shouts of rescue release my
　　　breakthrough. (Ps. 32:1–7 TPT)

I encourage you to stay consistent with this process of identifying a boulder, confessing, accepting forgiveness, and clearing a path. This is a great topic to revisit regularly in your two-way journaling sessions with the Lord. It's important not only for your heart but also for your family, your congregation, and the church at large. Boulders seep into songs, but clear roads do too!

Identity

One of the best ways to keep your songwriting roads clear of boulders is to know your identity.

The definition of *identity* is the "condition or character as to who a person or what a thing is; the qualities, beliefs, etc., that distinguish or identify a person or thing."[1]

I had a God moment in the middle of the night recently. I had been processing what identity was and had been writing about it the previous day. I asked God to give me more insight, and I heard Him whisper through the dark, "Identity is the definition of the heart." I sat straight up in bed.

You can't get more vulnerable than when your heart is seen for what it is. That's why identity is such a sensitive subject. That's why it's an important subject. It's the explanation of who we are at the deepest level. And while we are given identity as well as purpose by the hand of God, sometimes our choices, the influence of others, circumstances, or the enemy can confuse or cloud it. It's part of living here on this earth. The struggle is real.

How can we remember who we are? The One who hardwired us has all the answers, and He is eager to remind us. Knowing who we are matters because our identity is the foundation of every aspect of life, including our songwriting. It's the place we live from.

We search for our identity, don't we? Sometimes we look in all the wrong places. See if you can relate to this:

There once was a girl who tried on identities as she would try on clothing. She would look for what was fashionable at the time. She wanted to be a trendsetter. Sometimes she felt awkward in what she tried on, but she wore it anyway. Many times she would try on an outfit and then ask friends what they thought about it. Was it flattering? Was it her color? Their opinions mattered a lot to her, and she often made decisions based on what they thought was right for her. She surely could deal with something that was a little too tight. She could continue to retuck and reconfigure outfits as long as she looked good. Appearance trumped comfort.

Little did she know, there was a custom-made outfit hanging in the back of her closet. She couldn't see it because it was hidden by the mess of all her other outfits. This outfit was comfort at its best. In fact, you know those outfits that feel like pajamas and you feel as if you're cheating? This was it. Once she found it, that's all she ever wanted to wear.

Have you ever felt like this? Looking to others, the culture, and the trends will always cloud our identity. The only way to find our true identity is to look up.

> Your old life is dead. Your new life, which is your *real* life—even though invisible to spectators—is with Christ in God. *He* is your life. When Christ (your real life, remember) shows up again on this earth, you'll show up, too—the real you, the glorious you. Meanwhile, be content with obscurity, like Christ.
>
> And that means killing off everything connected with that way of death: sexual promiscuity, impurity, lust, doing whatever you feel like whenever you feel like it, and grabbing whatever attracts your fancy. That's a life shaped by things and feelings instead of by God. It's because of this kind of thing that God is about to explode in anger. It wasn't long ago that you were doing all that stuff

and not knowing any better. But you know better now, so make sure it's all gone for good: bad temper, irritability, meanness, profanity, dirty talk.

Don't lie to one another. You're done with that old life. It's like a filthy set of ill-fitting clothes you've stripped off and put in the fire. Now you're dressed in a new wardrobe. Every item of your new way of life is custom-made by the Creator, with his label on it. All the old fashions are now obsolete. Words like Jewish and non-Jewish, religious and irreligious, insider and outsider, uncivilized and uncouth, slave and free, mean nothing. From now on everyone is defined by Christ, everyone is included in Christ.

So, chosen by God for this new life of love, dress in the wardrobe God picked out for you: compassion, kindness, humility, quiet strength, discipline. Be even-tempered, content with second place, quick to forgive an offense. Forgive as quickly and completely as the Master forgave you. And regardless of what else you put on, wear love. It's your basic, all-purpose garment. Never be without it. (Col. 3:3–14)

And therein lies the struggle—flesh versus spirit. Discovering our identity requires looking up and choosing spirit over flesh time and time again.

As I researched identity in the Bible, I was surprised that many times when it's mentioned, it clearly comes in two parts. See if you can find what I did.

- "From now on everyone is defined by Christ, everyone is included in Christ" (Col. 3:11).
- "No matter how significant you are, it is only because of what you are a part of" (1 Cor. 12:20).
- "You are Christ's body—that's who you are! You must never forget this. Only as you accept your part of that body does your 'part' mean anything" (v. 27).
- "It's obvious by now, isn't it, that Christ's church is a complete Body and not a gigantic, unidimensional Part? It's not all Apostle, not all Prophet, not all Miracle Worker, not all Healer, not all Prayer in Tongues, not all Interpreter of Tongues. And yet some of you keep competing for so-called 'important' parts" (vv. 29–31).

Did you see the two parts of identity? Who we are in Him and who we are to the body.

So, yes, our personal identity comes from God. But we also have a part to play in His family. It's the other half of our identity. You could be completely confident in who you are individually in Christ and who He made you to be but still not be completely you until you are operating as part of the body. He made you to be inside the body.

If we look at the human body as an example, it helps us understand. One part, the heart, is a vital structure. We can identify the heart as the organ that pumps oxygen-filled blood to the rest of the body. It's the only organ that does this; its purpose is very specific. If the heart stops working, the body will not function either.

Did you know that a heart can beat on its own outside the chest? According to Dr. Christopher Magovern, "As remarkable as this seems, it can happen. Your heart has its own electrical system that causes your heart to beat, and as long as your heart continues to receive oxygen, it will continue to beat ... even if it's separated from the rest of your body."[2]

Yes, it's true. A heart can continue to function for a while outside the body. But it was created to beat inside the body. What would be the point of a heart beating outside? It has to be part of the body to function at its fullest. Not only will the heart benefit and continue to live when inside the body, but all other parts of the body benefit as well.

Without plugging in, we are missing belonging and purpose.

As I was two-way journaling one day, the Lord surprised me with a conversation about identity. It gave me new insight and a new perspective.

Conversation with the Lord

Me: Who am I to You, mighty God? How beautiful is Your covenant to me, Your promises to my frail heart. You are strength and life in a desert world. Who can find water, rivers, and streams besides You?

Him: You carry buckets for Me. You take water from the streams of life and take it to places where there is none. You are My beloved water girl. You waste no time in coming back to fill up your bucket.

You see need and you rush to it. Sometimes you get tired from all the serving, and you should rest. It's hard for you to rest when you see such great need.

Some people appreciate the water so much. Others have dumped it out in front of you. But I want you to know you're not responsible for the water being received well. You're just responsible to take it. Too many times you've taken on false responsibility. But it's false. The water comes from Me; you are a carrier.

Me: Lord, what is the water?

Him: The water is truth.

Me: What is the bucket?

Him: Your song. It contains My truth. How it's received will fall on Me, not on you. Remember, you are a carrier. But you always need to come back to the stream to fill up your bucket. You are a carrier who contains and delivers truth.

Finding our identity can be a process. I believe we all carry water, but our water may come from different parts of the stream. Our water could be healing, hope, joy, peace, reconciliation, wisdom, hospitality, compassion, mercy, grace, understanding, goodness, kindness, patience, faithfulness, or many other kinds.

Not only do we carry various kinds of water, but we have many different buckets as well. Your bucket could be marketing, painting, teaching, dancing, speaking, accounting, archaeology, medicine, customer service, cooking, technology, or songwriting.

Two-Way Journaling Time

Let's pause for a minute and see what the Lord has to say about your identity, specifically about who you are and how you fit into the body. You can use two-way journaling to see if you can get closer to the definition of your heart.

Ask the Lord these questions on paper; then listen with your pen.

1. What water am I carrying?
2. What is my bucket?

I believe our identity as individuals will be similar to our identity as writers. Truth is a big part of me, so it makes sense that it would be a big part of my calling as a songwriter. When I create, many times I leave fingerprints of truth. You will leave fingerprints of your identity too.

There have been times I've heard a new song on the radio and absolutely known which of my friends had written it. The fingerprints gave it away. If your identity is clear, your songs will show it. If you are unsure of who you are, your songs will show that too. This is another good reason to continue the process of discovering your identity.

We have talked about how important it is that heart comes first when writing worship songs. We know true worship is born at the crossroads of honesty, love, discipline, and sacrifice. Reading God's Word and praying are so helpful in keeping us there, along with two-way journaling. All of us experience boulders along the way, and keeping those clear from our paths is a process but well worth it.

Knowing your identity—who you are in Him and who you are to the body—is essential in the boulder-clearing process.

Next, you will learn more about some important skills of song-writing. As you learn about these skills, don't forget about building your heart! Continue spending time with the Lord, getting your daily bread by reading God's words and two-way journaling. He has more to say to you—and through you.

6

Understanding Your Songwriter Personality

Be yourself; everyone else is already taken.
Author Unknown

Many of us have done lots of personality tests, like the Enneagram, helping us understand ourselves and those around us. We may have done a spiritual gifts test or a fivefold ministry test to see how we best fit into the body of Christ. But have you ever thought about your songwriter personality?

After many writing sessions, especially cowriting sessions, I began noticing patterns of behavior, creativity, and instinct in myself and others. I began to identify early in songwriting sessions which type of writer my cowriters were. I would subconsciously categorize them in order to know how to best work with them.

I began thinking thoughts such as *He likes to talk; he's gotta be strong in content … She's an internal processor … He needs to sing that melody out loud in order to hear how he feels about it … He is listening to me even if he doesn't respond because he is calculating.*

Over time I created the Songwriter Personality Test. I am excited to share this free tool with you.

The Songwriter Personality Test is game changing for two reasons. First, if we know our identity as songwriters and what our greatest strengths are, we gain great confidence in our writing. We learn about our nature. We learn where we can soar and where we need to grow.

Second, we learn how we fit into the bigger picture with others. This will be vital when we begin to talk about the musical expression of community: cowriting. We will continue to reference this chapter throughout that process. I truly believe that God made the body to operate in fullness together in songwriting. When we each bring our strengths, the outcome is beautiful. This will take the pressure off you and keep you from needing to do it all yourself. When we put great gifts together, each person contributes his or her strength, and amazing songs are written.

"Are you a melody person or a lyric person?" I've been asked this question so many times that I thought all writers fit into one of those two categories. But eventually I saw there were more. In fact, I saw seven. So if you don't feel as if you fit into either the lyric or the melody category, you may be relieved to hear that.

The seven possible songwriter personality types are these:

1. Content
2. Hearing/Prophetic
3. Concept
4. Structure
5. Melody
6. Producer/Track
7. Chords/Arranging

Let me say up front, no one gift is better than another. Remember what we read in the previous chapter about competing for the so-called important gifts (see 1 Cor. 12:31)? We need every one.

You can spend five to seven minutes now taking the test, and then we will explore all the personality types and how they operate. If you have more time, I highly recommend printing the extended test and tallying all your scores so you can see what your top two categories are.

Also, please know that this test was written assuming previous cowriting experience. If you've never cowritten, simply answer these questions based on how you think you'd respond. You should still get a fairly accurate answer.

Take the test now! Go to the "Take the Test" tab on the Krissy Nordhoff website (www.krissynordhoff.com/test).

Which type of songwriter are you? Before we analyze each personality, I want to show you a diagram of the bigger picture. All these personality types can fit into one of three categories: *Lyrics*, *Craft*, or *Music*.

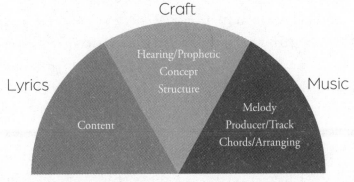

The *Lyrics* category is made up of our Content writers. Their main focus is many times not musical at all. In fact, it's the other side of the spectrum: they love words!

The *Craft* category is made up of those with the following songwriter personalities: Hearing/Prophetic, Concept, and Structure. As you can see, these are in the center of the diagram. While craft is their first gift, their second gift will usually lean toward lyrics *or* music. Remember I mentioned it was a good idea to take the extended test to find out your second gift? This is why. If you are in the center of the diagram, you will need to know which way you lean.

The *Music* category contains those with the gifts of Melody, Producer/Track, and Chords/Arranging. This side of the diagram leans away from *Lyrics*.

Take a moment to notice where you are on the diagram. If your songwriter personality falls under *Craft*, check to see what your second gift is so you know which direction you will tend to lean. Sometimes you will need to consider your third gift for more clarity.

When we talk about cowriting, we will view this diagram as a scale. Whichever side your gift is on, you will want to add weight to the opposite side to create balance. Working with others who have different strengths makes the cowriting process much more enjoyable, and the songs are usually stronger as well. In my opinion, the ideal number is three different strengths or gifts in the room. Be aware that working with someone with similar gifts could cause conflict in the writing room.

Now, let's take a closer look at each gift so that you better understand not only yourself as a writer but also those you will be writing with.

Content Writers

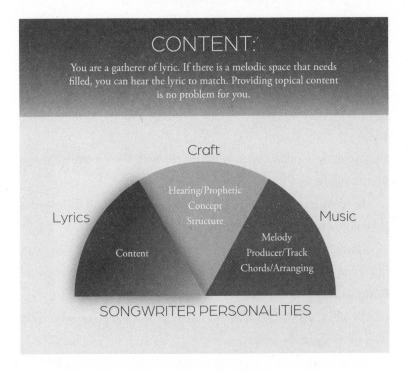

CONTENT:

You are a gatherer of lyric. If there is a melodic space that needs filled, you can hear the lyric to match. Providing topical content is no problem for you.

Craft

Hearing/Prophetic
Concept
Structure

Lyrics

Content

Music

Melody
Producer/Track
Chords/Arranging

SONGWRITER PERSONALITIES

If you are a Content writer, you scored highest on these characteristics:

1. You have many unfinished verses or chorus pieces.
2. When choosing between talker and listener, most people would say you are a talker.
3. When you hear a song written by someone else, you have a lot of fun adding your own verses or chorus lyrics.
4. Having a good melody is important, but what the song is saying matters most.
5. If you don't have a lyrical hook to build the song around, you have a very hard time moving ahead.

Content writers are gatherers of lyric. They are very conversational, both in and out of the writing room. They usually love the spoken word. Sometimes you will see them scribbling song ideas during sermons as they are inspired by the spoken word. Many times they have collections of title ideas. If there is a melodic space that needs to be filled, they can hear the lyric to match. They are great at getting things started and keeping things going in a writing session.

Strength: Content writers are overflowing with words! There is no such thing as a lyric shortage.

Challenge: They need to be careful to make sure all these words stay on track with the goal for the song.

Best-case cowriting scenario: Content writers work best with one *Craft* writer (Hearing/Prophetic, Concept, Structure) and one *Music* writer (Melody, Producer/Track, Chords/Arranging).

Possible cowriting conflict: Content writers should avoid writing with other Content writers.

In situations where working with one writer from the *Craft* category and one from the *Music* category is not possible, it may work to write with two types of *Craft* writers or two types of *Music* writers.

Hearing/Prophetic Writers

If you are a Hearing/Prophetic writer, you scored highest on these characteristics:

1. You feel less like a songwriter or worship leader and more like a messenger of truth.

2. When you focus on writing for congregational purposes, you would rather write about how you anticipate God will move in the future than about what He is doing right now.

3. You have experienced the miraculous when praying for others.

4. You are not as interested in theology as you are in hearing God's voice personally.

5. You need to express your ideas verbally, especially where matters of right and wrong are involved.

6. You have a natural desire for justice.

7. You are completely comfortable with a free-flow song with little structure.

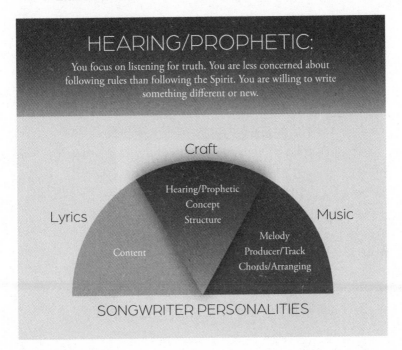

HEARING/PROPHETIC:
You focus on listening for truth. You are less concerned about following rules than following the Spirit. You are willing to write something different or new.

Craft

Hearing/Prophetic
Concept
Structure

Lyrics

Music

Content

Melody
Producer/Track
Chords/Arranging

SONGWRITER PERSONALITIES

These writers don't necessarily focus on either lyrics or melody, although they may lean one way or the other. They focus on listening. They love truth. They feel responsible for delivering an accurate message. They are less concerned about following rules than following the Spirit and are always willing to write something different or new. They love spontaneity.

Strength: Hearing/Prophetic writers are great at keeping things fresh!

Challenge: They need to be careful not to push the congregation too far past their comfort zone in worship.

Best-case cowriting scenario: Hearing/Prophetic writers work best with a Content writer from the *Lyrics* category and a writer from the *Music* category.

Possible cowriting conflict: Hearing/Prophetic writers should avoid writing with other Hearing/Prophetic writers.

In cases where a *Lyrics* and *Music* combination of writers is not available, simply choose writers who have different gifts from yours. Look at your second gift and see which direction you lean.

If your second gift is in the *Lyrics* category, lean the opposite way.

Here are possible combinations:

- Concept writer plus any Music personality
- Structure writer plus any Music personality
- Any two different *Music* personalities

If your second gift is in the *Music* category, lean the opposite way.

Here are possible combinations:

- Content and Concept
- Content and Structure

These combinations could also work well if your second gift is in the Music category:

- Concept plus one of the *Music* gifts (make sure this gift is different from your second gift)
- Structure plus one of the *Music* gifts (make sure this gift is different from your second gift)

Concept Writers

CONCEPT:
You are a storyteller. You excel at seeing and mapping out the big picture of where the song needs to go.

Craft

Hearing/Prophetic
Concept
Structure

Lyrics

Music

Content

Melody
Producer/Track
Chords/Arranging

SONGWRITER PERSONALITIES

If you are a Concept writer, you scored highest on these characteristics:

1. You like to tell stories.
2. You are a big-picture person; details do not appeal to you.

3. Sometimes you get ideas for the direction of a song, but you don't necessarily like to figure out the lyrics to describe it.
4. You love setting goals and casting vision.
5. You are usually the one in the writing room who is able to explain the lyrical target.

These are the storytellers. They are savvy at mapping out the big picture of where the song needs to go and keeping it cohesive. They help make sure all the details that come out during the writing session fit into the overall theme of the song. They are goal focused. They are the guardrails.

Strength: Concept writers are great at determining which ideas will strengthen the song.

Challenge: They need to leave room for ideas to develop through brainstorming. Sometimes an idea has to go through several stages before it blossoms.

Best-case cowriting scenario: Concept writers work best with a Content writer from the *Lyrics* category and a writer from the *Music* category.

Possible cowriting conflict: Concept writers should avoid writing with other Concept writers.

In cases where a *Lyrics* and *Music* combination of writers is not available, simply choose writers who have different gifts from yours. Look at your second gift and see which direction you lean.

If your second gift is in the *Lyrics* category, lean the opposite way.

Here are possible combinations:

• Hearing/Prophetic plus any *Music* personality
• Structure plus any *Music* personality
• Any two different *Music* personalities

If your second gift is in the *Music* category, lean the opposite way. Here are possible combinations:

- Content plus Hearing/Prophetic
- Content plus Structure

These combinations could also work well if your second gift is in the Music category:

- Hearing/Prophetic and one of the *Music* gifts (make sure this gift is different from your second gift)
- Structure and one of the *Music* gifts (make sure this gift is different from your second gift)

Structure Writers

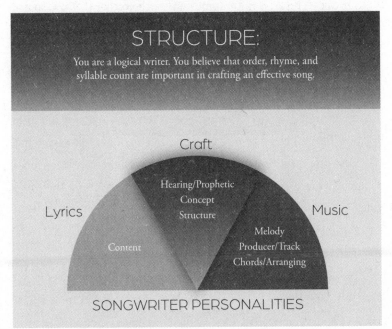

STRUCTURE:

You are a logical writer. You believe that order, rhyme, and syllable count are important in crafting an effective song.

Craft

Lyrics

Hearing/Prophetic
Concept
Structure

Music

Melody
Producer/Track
Chords/Arranging

Content

SONGWRITER PERSONALITIES

If you are a Structure writer, you scored highest on these characteristics:

1. You view songwriting like a puzzle. Sometimes moving the pieces makes all the difference.
2. You love to organize, and everything must have its place.
3. You notice and suggest switching lines or the order of verses so they make more sense or have more impact.
4. You like to start out with the weaker lines or verses and build to the strongest.
5. You love meter—syllables of each line need to match exactly, or it drives you crazy.

Structure writers are logical writers. They believe that order, rhyme, and syllable count are very important in crafting song. They like creativity, but it is more important to them that the lyric makes sense and progresses and that the transitions and sections feel natural. They love patterns and thrive on completing them.

Strength: Structure writers are consistent in their writing, and their patterns are easily followed by congregations.

Challenge: They need to stay open to concepts that may not fit in the box (like not using perfect rhymes). Irregularities can be awesome!

Best-case cowriting scenario: Structure writers work best with a Content writer from the *Lyrics* category and a writer from the *Music* category.

Possible cowriting conflict: Structure writers should avoid writing with other Structure writers.

In cases where a *Lyrics* and *Music* combination of writers is not available, simply choose writers who have different gifts from yours. Look at your second gift and see which direction you lean.

If your second gift is in the *Lyrics* category, lean the opposite way. Here are possible combinations:

- Hearing/Prophetic plus any *Music* personality
- Concept plus any *Music* personality
- Any two different *Music* personalities

If your second gift is in the *Music* category, lean the opposite way. Here are possible combinations:

- Content plus Hearing/Prophetic
- Content plus Concept

These combinations could also work well if your second gift is in the Music category:

- Hearing/Prophetic and one of the *Music* gifts (make sure this gift is different from your second gift)
- Concept and one of the *Music* gifts (make sure this gift is different from your second gift)

Melody Writers

If you are a Melody writer, you scored highest on these characteristics:

1. You feel unsettled in writing until you land a musical hook.
2. When you write songs, you always hear the melody first.
3. You love to hum or whistle.
4. When you listen to new songs, you get pumped most when you hear a fresh melody, and you sing it for days even though you don't necessarily remember the words.

5. When writing, you often use nonsense words to fill the spaces until you can go back and think about the lyric.

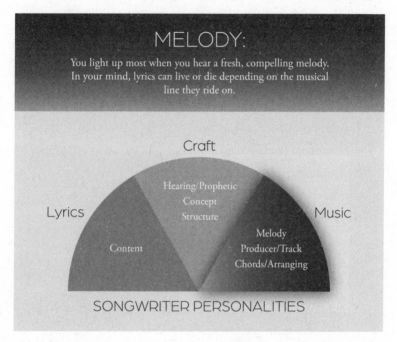

These writers light up most when they hear a fresh, compelling melody. In the Melody writer's mind, the strength of the lyrics depends on the musical line they ride on. Sometimes Melody writers may not be able to tell you the lyrics to some of their favorite songs because their focus is melody. In a cowriting session, the melodic hook is the North Star that guides them. Their songs are always memorable because of them.

Strength: Melody writers add so much color and interest to songs and power to the lyrics with the movement of their melodies.

Challenge: They need to make sure the lyrics are just as strong as the melody. The marriage of both makes the best songs.

Best-case cowriting scenario: Melody writers work best with a Content writer from the *Lyrics* category and a writer from the *Craft* category.

Possible cowriting conflict: Melody writers should avoid writing with other Melody writers.

In cases where a *Lyrics* and *Craft* combination of writers is not available, simply choose writers who have different gifts from yours. Look at your second gift and see which direction you lean.

If your second gift is in the *Lyrics* category, bring balance with a *Craft* personality. Here are some possible combinations:

- Any two different *Craft* personalities
- Hearing/Prophetic plus Producer/Track
- Hearing/Prophetic plus Chords/Arranging
- Concept plus Producer/Track
- Concept plus Chords/Arranging
- Structure plus Producer/Track
- Structure plus Chords/Arranging

If your second gift is in the *Craft* category, here are some possible combinations:

- Content and Producer/Track
- Content and Chords/Arranging
- Content and one of the *Craft* gifts (make sure this is different from your second gift)
- Producer/Track and one of the *Craft* gifts (make sure this is different from your second gift)
- Chords/Arranging and one of the *Craft* gifts (make sure this is different from your second gift)

Producer/Track Writers

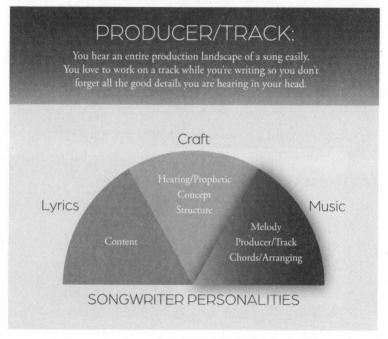

PRODUCER/TRACK:

You hear an entire production landscape of a song easily. You love to work on a track while you're writing so you don't forget all the good details you are hearing in your head.

Craft

Hearing/Prophetic
Concept
Structure

Lyrics

Music

Melody
Producer/Track
Chords/Arranging

Content

SONGWRITER PERSONALITIES

If you are a Producer/Track writer, you scored highest on these characteristics:

1. When you are in a cowriting session, you can easily get lost for a while in track-building land.
2. When you hear a melody, you can automatically hear many other parts and determine where they all need to go.
3. You can state your top three guitar sounds right now.
4. You have been inspired in the past by certain sounds, and you love to reinvent them as you build a track.
5. An OK song can sound amazing if it has the right treatment.

Producer/Track writers hear an entire landscape of a song. When writing a song, they love to work on a track at the same time so they don't forget all the layers of sounds they are hearing in their heads. They have been known to get "in the zone" as they focus. Many times their ideas inspire greater melodies and lyrics from the others in the room.

Strength: Producer/Track writers know how to use instrumentation to build feeling, intensity, and resolution in amazing ways. Many times it's the hooks (or motifs) that mark a song.

Challenge: Sometimes the Producer/Track zone can give them tunnel vision. They need to bear in mind what is happening with the others in the writing room.

Best-case cowriting scenario: Producer/Track writers work best with a Content writer from the *Lyrics* category and a writer from the *Craft* category.

Possible cowriting conflict: Producer/Track writers should avoid writing with other Producer/Track writers.

In cases where a *Lyrics* and *Craft* combination of writers is not available, simply choose writers who have different gifts from yours. Look at your second gift and see which direction you lean.

If your second gift is in the *Lyrics* category, bring balance with a Craft personality.

Here are possible combinations:
- Any two different *Craft* personalities
- Hearing/Prophetic plus Melody
- Hearing/Prophetic plus Chords/Arranging
- Concept plus Melody

- Concept plus Chords/Arranging
- Structure plus Melody
- Structure plus Chords/Arranging

If your second gift is in the *Craft* category, here are some possible combinations:
- Content and Melody
- Content and Chords/Arranging
- Content and one of the *Craft* gifts (make sure this is different from your second gift)
- Melody and one of the *Craft* gifts (make sure this is different from your second gift)
- Chords/Arranging and one of the *Craft* gifts (make sure this is different from your second gift)

Chords/Arranging Writers

If you are a Chords/Arranging writer, you scored highest on these characteristics:

1. During a cowriting session, you cannot move past a section of the song if it has the wrong chord.
2. Chord progression needs to be decided while the song is being written and cannot wait until the end of the writing session.
3. You love writing things in a creative way, like adding suspended or minor chords, to keep things interesting.
4. Songs with expected chord patterns have no appeal to you.
5. You think it would be fun to end a song on a chord other than the one chord.

CHORDS/ARRANGING:

You are always experimenting with new chords and chord progressions. When you are writing, you zero in on which chords would best support the melody in a fresh way.

Craft

Hearing/Prophetic
Concept
Structure

Lyrics

Music

Content

Melody
Producer/Track
Chords/Arranging

SONGWRITER PERSONALITIES

Chords/Arranging writers are always experimenting with new chords and chord progressions. While writing a song, their minds zero in on which chords would best support the melody in a fresh way. To them what really makes a song stand out—and what makes the melody unique—is a fresh placement of chords. They use the element of surprise as a way to keep interest throughout the song.

Strength: Chord/Arranging writers have the ability to craft chords that keep our interest throughout the song by using the unexpected in amazing, artistic ways.

Challenge: Learning to move past a chord so the cowriting can progress may be difficult but is sometimes needed. Keeping it simple is important in congregational worship.

Best-case cowriting scenario: Chords/Arranging writers work best with a Content writer from the *Lyrics* category and a writer from the *Craft* category.

Possible cowriting conflict: Chords/Arranging writers should avoid writing with other Chords/Arranging writers.

In cases where a *Lyrics* and *Craft* combination of writers is not available, simply choose writers who have different gifts from yours. Look at your second gift and see which direction you lean.

If your second gift is in the *Lyrics* category, bring balance with a *Craft* personality.

Here are possible combinations:
- Any two different *Craft* personalities
- Hearing/Prophetic plus Melody
- Hearing/Prophetic plus Producer/Track
- Concept plus Melody
- Concept plus Producer/Track
- Structure plus Melody
- Structure plus Producer/Track

If your second gift is in the *Craft* category, here are some possible combinations:
- Content and Melody
- Content and Producer/Track
- Content and one of the *Craft* gifts (make sure this is different from your second gift)
- Producer/Track and one of the *Craft* gifts (make sure this is different from your second gift)

- Melody and one of the *Craft* gifts (make sure this is different from your second gift)

If you would like to hear more about your songwriter personality, check out the interviews I did on each type with some professional songwriters. These conversations give amazing insight. You can find these by visiting www.krissynordhoff.com/book. This is a great resource for helping you understand how you think and why you are wired the way you are.

Now that you know who you are as a songwriter, where your natural abilities lie, some of your strengths and challenges, and whom you may pair well with in a cowriting situation, I would like to introduce you to some skill-building practices that will support you as you begin to create new songs!

7

Psalming

To have a heart like King David is to have a
heart that always returns to God.

Abbey Phipps

It occurred to me one day that the Psalms were meant to be sung, not simply read! They are songs, after all. I began to wonder what they may have sounded like. I put my Bible up on my piano and began to sing them, and I began learning from the patterns I saw in David's writing.

Honesty, love, discipline, sacrifice—David was in the very center of the crossroads. I saw choruses or refrains, structure, poetic devices, and so much more. I want to share a few things I've found.

I have learned more about the skill of writing worship songs by singing the Psalms aloud than through any other way. For the purpose of discussing this concept, I will refer to it as "psalming."

Format

One of my favorite aspects of psalming is the format I saw David using time and time again. There was an order to his worship. See if you can find it in this passage: "Don't turn a deaf ear when I call you, God. If all I get from you is deafening silence, I'd be better off in the Black Hole. I'm letting you know what I need, calling out for help and lifting my arms toward your inner sanctum.... Blessed be GOD—he heard me praying. He proved he's on my side; I've thrown my lot in with him. Now I'm jumping for joy, and shouting and singing my thanks to him" (Ps. 28:1–2, 6–7).

Do you see what I saw? It happens in many psalms. Here's the format:

1. David was in a tough place. Fear, sin, isolation— name it—he had been there. This is where he started many psalms.
2. David cried out. He called on the Lord, knowing he would be saved, even though it may take a long time.
3. The Lord heard and answered!
4. David worshipped.

This formula is important to remember when writing songs, especially worship songs. There is a place for songs that dive straight into worship. But hearing the process brings understanding as to how we get to that point of worship. Seeing the whole picture makes all the difference in the depth of our worship.

Call and Response

Psalm 136 looks like a call-and-response type of song. This form can be powerful. When a congregation sings this type of song, they don't need to look at the screen to know their response. Removing that step allows more room for thought about what is being sung. Many more worship songs are going back to this type of song. While it is an ancient idea, it is still relevant for today.

I love that while the "call" lines are in the past and present, the "response" lines are always in the present. This further underscores the unchanging nature of God.

Remembrance

Through this psalm we can also learn about the importance of telling the stories of what God has done. Songs are important reminders of history and God's faithfulness. This psalm starts with a simple call to thanks, declares His sovereignty, speaks of creation, tells how He rescued the Israelites, and recounts how He saved them from their enemies, takes care of every need, and does it all. In one song they have an amazing amount of detail about their history and victory with the Lord. What a beautiful way to make sure future generations remember.

> Thank GOD! He deserves your thanks.
>> *His love never quits.*
> Thank the God of all gods,
>> *His love never quits.*

Thank the Lord of all lords.
>*His love never quits.*

Thank the miracle-working God,
>*His love never quits.*

The God whose skill formed the cosmos,
>*His love never quits.*

The God who laid out earth on ocean foundations,
>*His love never quits.*

The God who filled the skies with light,
>*His love never quits.*

The sun to watch over the day,
>*His love never quits.*

Moon and stars as guardians of the night,
>*His love never quits.*

The God who struck down the Egyptian firstborn,
>*His love never quits.*

And rescued Israel from Egypt's oppression,
>*His love never quits.*

Took Israel in hand with his powerful hand,
>*His love never quits.*

Split the Red Sea right in half,
>*His love never quits.*

Led Israel right through the middle,
>*His love never quits.*

Dumped Pharaoh and his army in the sea,
>*His love never quits.*

The God who marched his people through the desert,
>*His love never quits.*

Smashed huge kingdoms right and left,
    His love never quits.
Struck down the famous kings,
    His love never quits.
Struck Sihon the Amorite king,
    His love never quits.
Struck Og the Bashanite king,
    His love never quits.
Then distributed their land as booty,
    His love never quits.
Handed the land over to Israel.
    His love never quits.

God remembered us when we were down,
    His love never quits.
Rescued us from the trampling boot,
    His love never quits.
Takes care of everyone in time of need.
    His love never quits.
Thank God, who did it all!
    His love never quits! (Ps. 136)

Refrain or Chorus

Psalm 99 is one of many psalms I have gotten excited about because it led me to understanding what David was intending musically for certain sections. When I see words repeated, for instance, I know the music would have repeated on those lines as well. (We would call them a refrain or a chorus today.) So, when I sing this psalm, I will sing those lines with the same melody every time.

The following psalm appears to be three verses, each followed by the same refrain or chorus. The first verse is a lyrical theme about where God rules from, followed by worship. The second verse is a reflection on who God is and a call to honor Him, followed by worship. The third verse is an explanation of how keeping God's laws brings His favor, followed by more worship. I love that each verse has a slightly different topic but they progressively get deeper. They move from God being on His angel throne to being someone we can understand and even interact with. There is a beautiful progression here. But the worship happens at every step.

> GOD rules. On your toes, everybody!
> He rules from his angel throne—take notice!
> GOD looms majestic in Zion,
> He towers in splendor over all the big names.
> Great and terrible your beauty: let everyone praise you!
> Holy. Yes, holy.

> Strong King, lover of justice,
> You laid things out fair and square;
> You set down the foundations in Jacob,
> Foundation stones of just and right ways.
> Honor GOD, our God; worship his rule!
> Holy. Yes, holy.

Moses and Aaron were his priests,

Samuel among those who prayed to him.

They prayed to GOD and he answered them;

He spoke from the pillar of cloud.

And they did what he said; they kept the law he
> gave them.

And then GOD, our God, answered them

(But you were never soft on their sins).

Lift high GOD, our God; worship at his holy mountain.

> Holy. Yes, holy is GOD our God. (Ps. 99)

Poetic Devices

There are some poetic devices used in the Psalms that we simply do not notice because of the language difference. Because of this, some of these devices can be found only by researching information on the Psalms. For instance, Psalm 4 contains an acrostic that, when read from bottom to top, spells "Unto a lamp for Zerubbabel." An acrostic is "a composition usually in verse in which sets of letters (such as the initial or final letters of the lines) taken in order form a word or phrase or a regular sequence of letters of the alphabet."[1] Did you know that Psalm 119 is also acrostic poetry? The first eight lines of the psalm all begin with the letter *aleph*, the first letter of the Hebrew alphabet. The next eight lines begin with *beth*, the second letter. And so on for 176 verses until we reach the end at the last letter, *taw*. No wonder the psalm is so long! Each of the letters must have its turn.

Some scholars believe this device was used to show completeness, as in complete devotion to the law of God.[2]

How amazing! What creativity and craft!

I am convinced there is no better way to learn how to write worship than through soaking up these psalms. I believe the Holy Spirit will bring insight in ways we cannot begin to understand as we sing them back to life. He is the best teacher I know. There is much more to be discovered—and much more you can discover through psalming.

Psalming Exercise

Let's try this! Grab your Bible now and open up to the Psalms. Choose any psalm or stanza to sing aloud as you imagine what melody King David used with those very words. The first time you sing the psalm aloud, try to sing through it word for word. Give yourself more freedom the second time. I promise there is no need for perfection. There is no need for an instrument (although that's an option). There is no need for production. This is simply you, a psalm, and melody. It doesn't have to sound good. Just sing!

Tips

For those of you who are Structure writers, singing straight through the psalm may be challenging for you. That's good! It's stretching you.

Many times, after I get past that first time through, I will go back and look for what I call my "anchor line." This line becomes sort of a refrain as I continue. I will sing a piece and go back to that anchor line, then sing another piece and go back to the anchor line again. This helps add a little structure. It feels more like a song to me that way.

Also, you can try approaching psalming as a prayer so you can feel less pressure to create structure.

For those of you who struggle with hearing melody, especially Content writers, here are a few things you can try:

- Sing the psalm to another melody you know if you have a hard time finding a new one.
- Play an instrumental soundtrack that you can sing over.
- Listen to another song in the background at a very low volume. Sing the melody you hear. If you play the song back at full volume, many times the melody you heard is much different, and it can spark great ideas.
- Study the inflections in people's voices when they speak. Listen to your voice when you speak the psalm out loud. Let your melody follow the same pattern. For instance, if you would raise the pitch of your voice when speaking, raise the melody there also.
- Begin to sing all the time! Sing in your car and when you're doing laundry; hum to yourself when you're in the grocery store. I believe this practice makes writing melody a part of everyday life and not something to fear when you sit down to psalm or write.
- If focusing on an entire psalm feels overwhelming, sing a small piece, only a few lines.
- If you're playing an instrument, keep the chording simple. Sometimes I choose two chords and play back and forth.
- Try out different vibes—upbeat, slow, etc.
- Switching up instrumentation may bring new inspiration. I recently bought a Seagull M4 dulcimer. It's much easier to play than a guitar, and I love it! If you're looking for an

instrument to try, a dulcimer is simple and fun. Most likely the psalms were played on stringed instruments too.

If you get to the point where you've gone through all the psalms, switch translations and do it again! You can visit the book tab on the Krissy Nordhoff website (www.krissynordhoff.com/book) to see some video examples of psalming.

Eventually you will find you get more and more ideas for songs of your own through psalming. It may start with one word or one phrase, but you will grow new songs from these moments. There are no better ideas than those tucked inside God's words. Chase those ideas!

Let's go! Try psalming now.

What did you think? What did you learn? I assure you that continuing this practice will grow you as a worship songwriter in amazing ways.

Many, many of the songs I have written that have been recorded by others have started out this way. In fact, by the time you read this, there will be one more! I usually start by myself at the piano or dulcimer in the morning, singing my psalms. Then I'll take bits and pieces into a cowriting session and end up coming out with another completely different song. Art inspires art; spirit stirs up spirit.

I hope psalming becomes a part of who you are, in skill and heart, as a songwriter. I highly encourage you to add it to your daily habits of reading God's words and journaling. Start slowly and build from there. Don't let yourself get overwhelmed. Try five minutes! Over time, if you'll commit to these small increments of time, it will become second nature.

8

Song Mapping, Roots, and Resources

A painter paints his pictures on canvas. But
musicians paint their pictures on silence.

Leopold Stokowski

Most of the time, songs begin with a word or phrase (lyrical or musical) that inspires. Recently I was psalming and came across these words that stood off the page to me: "Just like you promised" (Ps. 5:8 TPT). You may have had that feeling of something stirring your heart too. Some people get stuck right there because they are not sure what to do next. I get it and I've been there. Let me share something with you that I think can help.

I'd like to introduce you to song mapping, something I learned from Gloria Gaither, my songwriting professor at Anderson University.

Song mapping is a way for us to see on paper where we should go with our songs. It's a creative way to brainstorm and then organize our thoughts into related families. We always want to start by putting the big idea (usually the title) in the center of the page. This reminds us that everything else we write on that paper needs to be related to that main idea. It's our bull's-eye. In the example I mentioned above, I would write "Just Like You Promised" in the center of my paper.

Once you've got your main idea, you can start to brainstorm, writing related ideas around it. Here are a few ways to get started:

1. Ask questions such as "What has He promised?" "Whom did He promise it to?" and "How long will the promise last?"

2. You may also add some adjectives and adverbs that describe the promise, such as *faithful* and *forever*.

3. Think about some examples of God's promises, like God telling Abraham that his descendants would be as numerous as the stars in the sky and the grains of sand on the seashore (see Gen. 22:17).

Give yourself complete freedom to get your ideas out on paper. Then see if you can group those ideas into families. They should all clearly point to the main idea.

Brainstorming this way will help you see patterns. The patterns will help you organize your thoughts into verses, choruses, bridges, and eventually songs. A song will be much more cohesive with detailed and organized thought behind it if you think through the entire landscape on paper first.

If you'd like to see some examples of song mapping, visit the book tab on the Krissy Nordhoff website (www.krissynordhoff.com /book).

Ultimately the groupings can really help when it comes to shaping each section of the song. Here's the content we are looking for:

- verses: reasons, feelings, explanations, lists, details
- chorus: big idea, title, the "Why?" "Where?" "Who?" or "What?" answer to the verses
- bridge: "Why else?" with a twist, gives a deeper meaning to the chorus
- prechorus: a connecting piece, adds smoothness either lyrically or musically between what is presented in the verses and the chorus

Let's take a look at "Canyons," a song I wrote with Corey Voss, who also recorded it. I'm not going to show you a song map here, but I will show you where we were going with the content in each section. As you study the structure of various songs, you will begin to recognize these details more and more. That recognition is important when taking the content from song maps and shaping it into song. See what you see in the verses, chorus, and bridge:

Verse 1

Take me higher than the angels fly
Where there's freedom in the open sky
And my hope will never cease or die
Take me higher, Lord

Verse 2

Take me wider than the atmosphere
Where east and west just disappear
And my heart is open, free, and clear
Take me wider, Lord

Chorus
There is no limit to your endless love
Just when I doubt it, there is so much more
A rushing waterfall that overflows
It's filling canyons in my soul

Verse 3
Take me deeper than the ocean floor
I don't want the surface anymore
I am thirsty, God, and I am sure
Take me deeper, Lord

Bridge
And when you take me
Take all of me
I will not hold back
Anything[1]

Verses: The verses list different places, all telling us *where* we want to be taken. They all contain details and explanations.

Chorus: Here we find the answer to "Where?" It's God's love. It's the waterfall that fills our canyons. The chorus also tells us *why* we want to be there.

Bridge: The "taking" part of things gets deeper here as we give all of ourselves to God. It's a twist on the chorus because in the chorus He is giving us all of Himself. And in the bridge we are giving Him all of ourselves.

There's one more example I want to share with you. This is "Back to Life," a song I cowrote with Michael Farren and James Galbraith, recently recorded by Mandisa and by Anthony Evans.

Look at the verses, chorus, and bridge, and see if you think they contain the content that we want in each section of the song:

Verse 1

I breathe out confusion
I breathe in your truth
I breathe out all my fear
I breathe in your peace

Chorus

I, I'm coming back to life
I'm feeling hope arise
Because of you, only you, Jesus
I, I'm leaving the rest behind
My heart is satisfied
Because of you, only you, Jesus

Verse 2

I lay down my weakness
I take on your strength
I lay down my defenses
I step into your victory

Bridge
Resentment, depression and all anxieties
They have no power over me
Addiction and strongholds and every disease
They have no power over me[2]

Verses: The verses are lists.

Chorus: Here we clearly get an answer to "Why?" and it even says, "Because of you, only you, Jesus."

Bridge: The bridge is going deeper topically by naming the things we can get rid of because of Jesus. This is the twist.

Song Mapping Exercise

Let's try song mapping. If you have a collection of song ideas, pull one of them out. If not, think about the psalming we just did. Was there a phrase that stood out to you? There is no pressure here. You can use any word or phrase. There is no perfect way of song mapping and no exact science to it. It's meant to be idea fuel. In my experience it has been a helpful tool, especially to those just getting started. If you find yourself drifting from the map, follow your heart. The map has done its job and has given you ideas and direction.

Take the next few minutes to brainstorm your idea by song mapping. You can use the song mapping template below or find it under the book tab on the Krissy Nordhoff website (www.krissynordhoff .com/book).

Let's go! Try song mapping now.

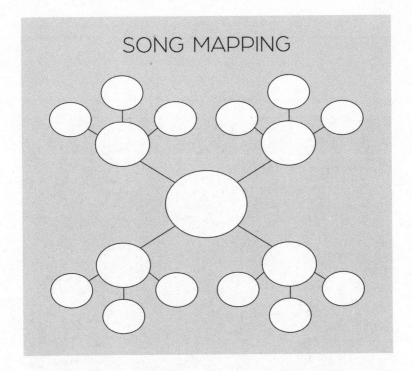

SONG MAPPING

How did it go? Did it help you to see all your thoughts on paper? Once you are done brainstorming, you can begin to group the content into verse, chorus, and bridge ideas. Use the descriptions in the previous section to help you categorize. Then, eventually you will move off the paper, add a melody, and see what happens! The melodies should feel like a natural connection to the lyrics. Keep shaping the two together until it feels like a fit.

Think of a song map like the root system of a tree. When we look at a tree, we usually cannot see the structure underneath, the support system. It's the same with a song. We don't really think about all this structure underneath. But that's exactly what adds stability, grounding, and support, enabling the song to grow, climb, and reach.

There are many other ways we can add support to our songs. Next, let's explore a few more roots!

Roots

Today I sat under this tree in my front yard and penned this poem: "The Mighty Leaning Oak."

They think they see it in complete
Every bit of majesty
The mystery of how it leans
The mighty leaning oak

The bark in layers, cracked and old
With mossy green between its folds
And branches high as clouds can go
The mighty leaning oak

Birds fly in from leaf to leaf
Flapping feathers, whistling beaks
It's every bit of home they seek
The mighty leaning oak

Sometimes acorns hang in rows
Like little men with hats exposed
A Christmas, in a solid gold
The mighty leaning oak

Heavy rain or greatest snow
Through broken twigs and icicles
Still candidly it grows and grows
The mighty leaning oak

But I'll tell you now what they can't see
It goes as high as it goes deep
Its strength is found beneath its feet
The mighty leaning oak

Roots hold tight to anchor down
They drink the water, feed the boughs
Life comes from the underground
The mighty leaning oak

The work in darkness and the dirt
Is never noticed, never heard
But yes, it matters; that's for sure
The mighty leaning oak

Do you hear the words it speaks?
"The secret lies in the unseen.
Just keep going, dear; you'll see …"
The mighty leaning oak

Tears began to stream down my face as I wrote the ending. The words paint such a picture of songwriting and life. My husband walked in on me crying, and we both laughed. But the words ring true.

People often love the fruit above ground, but to get it, you have to be OK with a little dirt.

Song mapping and other songwriting devices are the types of things that people either won't know about or probably won't notice when they hear your song. But should you choose to dig in and do the work to use them, they will create a more stable song.

Songwriting roots grow over time. Don't be overwhelmed by trying to learn them all. I suggest you incorporate one at a time as you begin to write songs. Learn to use each before you move on to another one.

These roots are tools professional songwriters know by heart and use on a regular basis, whether they know the technical names of them or not. But they too learned them one at a time.

Here is a quick reference guide for some of the most widely used "songwriting roots."

Lyrical Tools

Alliteration: Two successive words that begin with the same sound. For example, "Where feet may fail" from the song "Oceans."[3]

End rhyme: Rhyming the ends of lines. For example, "Amazing grace! How sweet the sound / That saved a wretch like me! / I once was lost, but now am found / Was blind, but now I see."[4]

Rhyming at the ends of lines helps those listening to feel a sense of resolution and rest. People also love to follow patterns with end rhyme. For example, you can rhyme sequential lines or every other line.

Internal rhyme: A rhyme involving a word in the middle of a line and a word at the end of that line. For example, "Sing a new song to Him who sits on" from "Revelation Song."[5]

End rhyme is great, but if you can also rhyme inside the line, even better!

Near rhyme: Rhyming in which the words sound similar but do not rhyme perfectly. For example, "You move with holy rage / In all

Your miraculous ways. / We simply stand here amazed" in "Fighting for Us."[6]

This is more and more the preferred method of rhyming. It sounds nice to the ear but doesn't sound too perfect.

Imagery: Descriptive or figurative language appealing to the senses. For example, "I've tasted and seen of the sweetest of loves" from "Holy Spirit."[7]

Some churches get tripped up on "feeling" words. Just be aware of your culture and context.

Simile: A figure of speech comparing one thing to a different thing by using *like* or *as*. For example, "Like a rose trampled on the ground" in "Above All."[8]

Personification: Giving human characteristics to something non-human. For example, "If the stars were made to worship" from "So Will I."[9]

Metaphor: A statement in which an object or action is applied to a word or phrase to which it is not literally applicable. Many times metaphors use the word *is* or *am*. For example, "I am a tree" in "How He Loves."[10]

Hyperbole: An exaggeration or overstatement. For example, "Reckless love of God" from "Reckless Love."[11]

Musical Tools

Prosody: Using music to support the lyric, especially to convey its emotion. For example, "A rushing waterfall" in "Canyons."[12]

Repetition: Musical symmetry or hooks that repeat. For example, the melody on "Who You are" in "Good, Good Father."[13]

Meter: The pattern of beats that establishes the structure and feel of a song. Most common meters are 4/4 as in "How Great Is Our God"[14] and 3/4 as in "In Christ Alone."[15] A 4/4 song can feel more like an anthem, whereas a 3/4 song can feel lighter or even more waltz-like.

Drone: Usually a one chord and a five chord played together or separately as an accompaniment. A drone sets the atmosphere and is sometimes played using a pad. "Pieces"[16] uses this tool.

Impact Tools

Contrast: Changing the rhythm, melody, timing, or another aspect can create great interest in a song. If the verse is very rhythmic, it's nice to contrast with a sparse chorus. If there are a lot of lyrics in the chorus, it's great to contrast with a less wordy bridge. Recently, worship songs have more contrast in voicing, changing from a male singer to a female singer. For example, the chorus versus the bridge in "No Longer Slaves."[17]

Space: Leaving room in the lyric line or melody line for processing thoughts and soaking in the song will only cause it to have greater impact. For example, notice the space in the chorus in "King of My Heart."[18]

Snowball: Always build from smallest to largest in terms of topic and music so that the greatest impact will be felt last, both in order of lines and in order of verses. For example, "Mercy Tree."[19]

Suspense: Using minor chords or keys can add suspense and a feeling of anticipation. For example, "Lead Me to the Cross."[20]

Octave punch: Many worship songs and worship leaders add emphasis and emotion by jumping up an octave near the end of a song. For example, "Lord, I Need You."[21]

Things to Watch For

Syllable emphasis: Make sure the way you emphasize syllables when you sing is the way you would emphasize them when you speak. Otherwise you are creating a distraction in your song.

Syllable count: As much as possible, craft matching syllable counts for matching lines. For instance, all four lines in a verse may have eight syllables apiece. You would then match up the second verse so it also has eight-syllable lines. When there is one line off, it can throw listeners off and make them feel unsure about what is happening or where the song is going. If you set an expectation, be sure to meet it.

Inversion: Otherwise known as "Yoda speak." This is acceptable for hymns, but for modern worship songs, it is not recommended. Lines such as "By his wounds we are healed" may be better understood by rephrasing as "We are healed by his wounds." So again, how you speak it is how you should sing it.

Pronouns: This is huge! Keep pronouns consistent throughout your song. It's really important because switching from *I* to *you*, for instance, can be confusing. It does happen in songs today, but there is usually some sort of transition line that clearly lets the listener know what is happening. It usually takes great skill to do that well. We will work toward that. But for starters, just keep pronouns consistent. Also, if *He* refers to Jesus, make sure it never refers to someone else.

That could get confusing and distracting as well. We want to remove as many possible distractions as we can before we share a song.

Resources

There are a few helpful tools to keep in mind as you begin gathering information for your song maps:

Google Docs (Docs.Google.com): If you have Gmail, then you have access to Google Docs. This is a great place to store lyrics, and you can share the document with others and see changes in real time when you cowrite. Google Docs etiquette: don't erase content from other writers or content you don't want to use unless you ask. (I learned this rule of songwriting from my friends Kenna West and Sue Smith. We almost made T-shirts about it one day.)

Dictionary.com and Thesaurus.com: When I'm looking for a word that means "surrender" but with a different rhyme or something that means "freedom" but not exactly, I use Thesaurus.com. If I can't remember whether a certain word always has a negative connotation or if I want more clarity on what a word means, I will check Dictionary.com.

RhymeBrain.com: This is a great rhyming resource. It's free and even has a songwriter helper setting.

BibleGateway.com: If a verse comes to mind while you are writing, always look it up! Read the passage it came from. All the content you need may be there.

Voice memos: Smartphones have a search feature in the voice memos app. If you title your songs as you record them, you can search to easily find them. Also, I have been titling my ideas as *"Ideas"* so when I search, I can find them all at once if I need one. (While you are writing, record any new section of the song right away. I can't tell you how many times I've written a bridge, sung the chorus, and forgotten the new bridge!)

Notes app: Use this app on your smartphone for song ideas. Keep one note specifically for your song ideas.

Storing songs: I recommend doing a voice memo and a Google Doc for every song you write. Attach them to an email and send it to yourself. Create a "Songs" folder in your email so you have everything in one place. This should give you plenty of storage and prevent loss.

Songspace: I also use a monthly song-cataloging service called Songspace. You can check it out at songspace.com. This service has lots more options.

Roots and resources definitely make a difference. Keep in mind, though, it's really important to let go of perfection. Let your creativity flow whenever it does; then go back when the moment has passed and reevaluate things. See what you can add strength to at that point. You will find a balance!

Songwriting Exercise

Now that you've seen the list of some of the basic roots and resources, I want to talk about a process you can follow to put them into practice.

If you have a list of song ideas or any words or phrases you loved from psalming, pull it out. If those ideas are in your phone, keep it handy. You will also need it to record a voice memo.

If you have a laptop, open up a fresh Google Doc in one tab, RhymeBrain.com in another tab, Dictionary.com in another tab, and BibleGateway.com in another tab. You may not need all these every time you write, but it helps to have them available.

Go ahead and start a song map by putting one of your ideas in the middle of your map. Begin to brainstorm. See if you can find the right content to start either a verse or a chorus (let's start simply).

Once you narrow that down, you will choose one lyrical, musical, or impact tool. Let's begin with alliteration, two successive words that begin with the same sound. Like *stormy seas*, *great glory*, *mighty miracles*. Get an idea for a couple of words that would fit the context of your main idea and that you might be able to work into the song.

For help in getting started with melody, refer to our psalming chapter. There are several ideas there. It may take trial and error, and that's OK. Keep trying until something emerges. Some people need to hear music to begin to sing melody. Some sing melody, and the music comes afterward. Some get lyrics first. There is no wrong way to start a song. In fact, you may find one way you like the best, or you may switch it up every time.

Feel free to reference your online resources as needed for research and rhymes. Play with melody and lyric, making sure to use your main idea and your songwriting root.

If you feel as if you're getting into a creative flow, don't stop to evaluate roots. You can always put down some roots when that flow stops.

Finish the song if desired. Some songs will be for practice, and that is OK! Repeat this process with the next root, and work your way down the list until you've experienced them all.

Working repeatedly through this process, one tool at a time, is a great way to learn these devices by practical application. Over time you will also have a great number of songs or song starts as a result!

9

Cowriting

Alone we can do so little. Together we can do so much.
Helen Keller

We can and do need to write by ourselves. It's an important part of our relationship with the Father. But writing together is our musical expression of community. We grow by experiencing new perspectives, and cowriting allows us to lean into the strengths of others and work as a team.

Cowriting is two or more people sitting down to write a song together. The most people I've written a song with is seven or eight. But I wouldn't recommend it! Different perspectives are good, but having too many can make the writing much more challenging.

My favorite scenario is three people in a cowriting session. That number brings different perspectives, but there's always a clear majority! Cowriting is definitely an art—something you learn.

Have you ever cowritten? Maybe you have a friend you've been writing with already. Maybe there is no one you know in your town who writes songs. If so, I want you to start thinking outside of what you may think is possible. Writing can happen in many ways, given today's technologies. There are more options every day.

Finding a Cowriter

I've received lots of questions from people who live outside Nashville about how to find a cowriter. My first thought is always *Start at your home church.* There may be others there asking themselves the same questions. Next, research your local area. Ask people in neighboring churches. Often worship leaders are great connectors to the creatives in their congregations. Also, think online. There is a mentoring opportunity that is a follow-up to this book, called the Worship Songwriter Mentorship. You can find it at www.krissynordhoff.com/mentorship. During the mentorship program, cowriters are assigned according to songwriter personalities. This is a great way to connect over the internet with a small group as well as individual writers while in the comfort of your own home. I also host live writers' events periodically. You can check my schedule for upcoming events at www.krissynordhoff.com/events. There is also a lot going on for worship leaders and writers over at www.braveworship.com. That's another great place to connect with others and plug in to community.

Cowriting and Songwriter Personalities

When considering cowriting partners, it is really important to look at songwriter personalities, not only personalities in general. I have been in situations where I thought it would be great to cowrite with good friends, only to find out later that we totally didn't gel in the writing room. I also have worked well with some people in the writing room whom I probably wouldn't hang out with on the weekend. While there are many factors involved in how a cowriting session goes and how well we work with others, the songwriter personality test can help in a big way. Feel free to send your friends to www.krissynordhoff.com/test to see what they get.

Do you remember what your songwriter personality is? If you need a memory jog about the details of your personality, take a moment to go back to the relevant section of chapter 6, "Understanding Your Songwriter Personality." You can use this information time and time again, especially when it comes to setting up cowriting sessions.

When you go to review that section, you'll see the "best-case cowriting scenario." This is the ideal combination of you plus two other songwriter personalities, which should set you up for success, combining three strengths.

You will also see the "possible cowriting conflict." Those listed there have the same gifting as you. Have you ever heard someone say, "She doesn't get along with her mother because they are exactly alike"? Well, the same can be true in a cowriting situation. When we have the same giftings, clashes can take the writing off course and down rabbit trails leading nowhere. This scenario also creates a deficiency because we are missing a third strength in the room.

There are other winning combinations listed should your best-case cowriting scenario not be an option, giving you several other possibilities to work with.

Advice for Every Type

As you are working with others, make sure you take some time to research their type tendencies. It's good to know these things ahead of time so you know what to expect.

Use the following information as a quick reference before walking into a cowriting session.

Content: Content writers are usually verbal processors. They will share many ideas aloud. If you're not a content writer, don't be intimidated or feel as if you need to keep up. This is how they are wired. Focus on your own area of gifting. Also, be patient with them. It may take them a while to sort through all the lyrics that run through their brains. To content writers, writing songs is sort of like pruning a garden. They first have to see what all is there before they begin cutting away.

Hearing/Prophetic: Let them sing. They usually hear in musical moments. Let the instrument play, and give them room to listen. They will be frustrated by repeated interruptions, as it stops their process. They need prayer and worship. If you give them a time of free-flow worship, they usually get a beautiful piece that can be crafted afterward. It's hard for them to try crafting first. It feels unnatural to them.

Concept: Bring all your content and all your melodies! You can throw anything out into the middle of the room. They are the gardeners. They know just how to trim and shape. Sometimes they are internal processors for a while, but they may be gathering information. When they verbalize their thoughts, they are clear and make a lot of sense. Trust their direction on the song and how they keep everything on target.

Structure: These writers are calmers of chaos. They turn lemons into lemonade. They will see the unexpected and make sure every line is shored up. They love details; don't let that frustrate you. You may be totally fine with a chorus that they are still not sure about. But these are the details that make great songs amazing. If you let them explore every last question during the writing session, later your song will be much more polished.

Melody: Often melody writers are inspired by beats or loops and chord progressions. Letting an instrument play for a little bit or playing a loop gives them plenty of room to create. Be careful not to fill all the space in the room with conversation, as it's harder for them to hear. Usually they are good at finding these little pockets of time themselves and then expressing their voice. If they start chasing a melody, let them finish!

Producer/Track: These writers have so many instrumental parts running through their heads. Expect that they need to get all those things down on the track before they forget them, even as you are writing. They will be listening to you, even if their backs are turned for a bit. They are good multitaskers. Trust that they hear you and that you will have an opportunity to discuss your thoughts. Meanwhile, be flexible in working on other things, such as verse 2 lyrics, until they reengage. They work in an ebb and flow.

Chords/Arranging: These writers will bring so much color to a song! They view songwriting as a treasure hunt. They like to stop at each location and find the "treasure" chord before they move on. When they are at one of these stops, simply understand they will need a little time. Work on lyrics or other ideas for a couple of minutes, or take the opportunity to go get a snack. When they find the right chord, they will be renewed and refreshed, ready to keep going. And you will be thrilled with the character their search added to the song.

Three Ways of Cowriting

I recently finished a song with Travis Cottrell and Ben Cantelon. We started out in the writing room and needed to finish up the bridge. Since Travis lives out of town, we emailed ideas and sent voice memos back and forth. Then we finished up with some texts and finally a phone call. This song holds my record for the greatest number of ways it was written. It's called "His Name Is Jesus,"[1] if you want to hear it!

There are basically three ways people cowrite: in person, over Skype or FaceTime, or via email or text.

Writing in person is probably the way most cowriting still happens. Writing in person gives you the benefit of clearly seeing nonverbal communication, which I believe is over 90 percent of communication.

Video technology makes writing at a distance possible in real time. I've used Skype and FaceTime on many occasions. Overall it works well when writing long distance. However, there can be lag time and technical issues, so plan a little extra time.

Email or text works too. I have written several songs with Michael Neale over email. We simply continue to shape the idea, sending it back and forth until it's complete. If you are an internal processor, this method may work well. You can even send voice memos these ways as well as lyric ideas. This does, however, take more time.

Deciding how you will write may depend on your cowriters and their locations and availability. But know there is flexibility. Just because you don't have people to write with in your area doesn't mean you can't cowrite.

How to Get Started

Most of the time when I sit down to cowrite, I take a good bit of time just getting to know my cowriters. I'll ask them questions about their hearts, their families, what God is doing in their lives, and what God is doing in their churches. This helps me understand where they are coming from and also gives me great direction for what we should write about.

Next, it's always wise to have three ideas to share. Bring a gift to the party, so to speak. An idea can be lyrical, as in a word, phrase, or verse. It can also be musical, as in one line of a melody. Or it could be both put together into a phrase, verse, or chorus. I wouldn't recommend bringing an entire song. Most of the time the original writer will have a hard time letting go of a lot of things, and the other writers feel as if they don't have much to contribute.

Take a little time to share ideas. Be mindful of how much time each writer spends sharing so you can make time for everyone. Keep in mind that you will need to go deep in your conversation pretty quickly, but please don't allow the time to turn into a counseling session. I cannot overstate that. People do care, but they also get frustrated when you've shared for two hours, there is one hour left, and there's not much time to write anything. We need to be able to cycle back to the goal after sharing and make sure there is time to write a song.

Inevitably there will be one idea that resonates well with everyone. Chase that one. Don't be offended if your ideas aren't chosen. You want them to be chased with excitement, and the next cowriting session may be the right one to bring them to. There's nothing worse than feeling that someone is going to push his or her agenda no matter how others in the room feel about it.

After you've agreed on an idea, worship with it for a bit. Play the idea or phrase until it sinks in. Write from response, not from striving. Let the exchange of ideas begin. Continue throwing out thoughts and possibilities. Be courageous. Don't be fearful in your sharing. Remember, some people will be internal processors and some will be external. You can ask them which they are, which may help you know what to expect. If your idea isn't connecting, throw out another one. It's a lot like baseball: the pitcher doesn't stop pitching just because someone doesn't hit the ball; he keeps pitching till there's a hit.

Let the Lord and the song lead you. I have seen one section of a song start out as a chorus, then become a verse, and finally ended up making a pretty good bridge! If you don't try to control the song, it will be able to change and grow in the best way. Be flexible! Dave Clark says, "Don't be in such a rush to find a song in everything that you don't leave room for the song to find you."

Make sure you write down your cowriters' contact information, as well as the date of creation and their publishing information.

If you have changes you'd like to make once the writing session is finished, you need to ask all involved if they are also OK with those changes.

Legally, if you brought in a piece of a song and you were unhappy with how the song finished, you can completely start over with the piece you brought in. Just be sure to ask the others who worked on the song if they are OK with you writing a completely different version of it.

Regardless, in any situation you are unsure of, *communicate*! You can't overcommunicate.

When you are finished, get a good work tape on your smartphone and a lyric. Put them together in an email, send it to yourself, and put it in a *"Songs"* folder in your email.

If you enjoyed the cowriting, nurture the relationship. Write again soon! If it was tough, don't take it personally. Look for a new cowriting relationship.

Cowriting Tips

Making others feel safe is an important part of cowriting. The more safe that people feel, the more expressive they are able to be with their thoughts and feelings. But it's also important that you be honest. The give-and-take is a fine line. Here are a few tips that may be helpful as you begin to learn the art of cowriting. I hope they give you a leg up on writing etiquette, as well as insight into how to foster a safe environment in the room.

Do not feel as if the creativity comes from or depends on you. That's too much pressure. All creativity comes from the Creator. Your job is to listen.

Having a male and a female voice in the same song—or diversity through other combinations of perspectives—gives us a clearer picture of God's view.

Be gracefully true to yourself. Deliver your feelings, but do so in a kind and generous way.

Be confident in your voice, be it sensitive and nurturing or brave and bold, because it's a reflection of God in you unlike in anyone else. The rest of us get to see Him in a new way when you speak.

Before you go into a cowriting session, pray that you will not emotionally shut down because of what someone says or doesn't say. We want affirmation from others, but sometimes we hear accusation and that shuts us down.

Be authentically you. If you're not who you really are in a cowriting session, you will never write the songs God intended for you to write.

Understand that others may process information differently than you do and neither way is wrong. Before the cowriting begins, ask each writer how he or she likes to process. Study processing so you make the best use of your time and their time. Fast processing doesn't mean better processing.

Persistence is the difference. The people who have long-standing careers in the songwriting world are the people who were told no thousands of times and didn't give up. According to Michael Farren, "Songwriting is the only profession where a 90 percent failure rate is considered great success."

Relationship always trumps songs. No song is worth fighting over. You *will always* write more songs, but you might not always be able to repair a relationship.

Be generous with percentages. Assume you are splitting evenly, no matter what you bring in.

Never put yourself in a compromising position. Dress appropriately. Create a code word and share it with those close to you in case you ever need help. For instance, I have a word that both my publisher and my husband know is my code word. If I ever feel unsafe and text that word to them, they will be on their way to where I am ASAP.

Always cheer on your fellow songwriters; be quick to congratulate and celebrate them. Jealousy is the thief of joy. Crush a competitive spirit with a compliment.

Realize that the music industry is subjective, and don't let it dictate your dreams or your decisions more than the voice of God does. Work with people who see your greatness and are willing to remind you of it.

If you have children, that doesn't mean giving up on your dreams. You are now simply a role model for how to follow them.

You will learn something from every cowriting session. If you leave feeling as if an idea you brought in didn't turn out the way you'd hoped, that theme will come out in a better way on another song or you can always rewrite. Remember, great lines that came during the session but weren't used can be tucked away and used in other songs. Nothing is ever wasted!

Sometimes the Holy Spirit will choose to speak through one main person in a cowriting session. Be OK with that not being you.

Leave room for the Holy Spirit in the writing session. Let there be space in conversation for Him to speak.

If you are writing worship, don't forget to worship!

Cowriting should be fun, so make sure you laugh. (I've been known to pull pranks with rubber chickens every now and then!) If the writing session feels stuck—change something. Take a break; get a snack; take a walk; move to a different section of the song.

On that note, fun is definitely a big part of building relationships. Michael Farren has a bell in his studio. If you come up with a great line, you get to ring the bell. But he doesn't always agree with me, so now I carry my own bell in my writing bag so I can ring it anytime. When I first started writing with Dustin Smith, he didn't like a couple of my lines, so I started throwing jelly beans at him. Jelly beans turned into chocolate. Now I always have chocolate with me, especially when I write with Dustin!

I also write a lot with Zach Kale and Mike Grayson. We have found that when we get stuck, it's only because we need to walk across the street and get some "Holy Spirit fries." So far it has worked every time! On "Watch What He Will Do," the bridge came right after three orders!

Spirit in Cowriting

Out of the abundance of the heart the mouth speaks.
Matthew 12:34 ESV

Sometimes a writing session goes wrong, even when you're writing with the best combination of personality types. That's because something else can have an impact on cowriting. That something else is the attitude and outlook someone walks in with. Many times we can hear the spirit of someone's heart through that person's words. Just as lyrics have impact, spoken words do as well. Spoken words can usher in a spirit of pride and division or a spirit of holiness, kingdom, and much more.

I urge you to choose your words wisely when you cowrite so that the spirit in the room remains encouraging and open to new ideas. I've heard it said that a no spoken in any form will shut down creativity. Some of you have cowritten more, but it's still new to some of you. Consider these ideas for phrasing your feelings in a healthy way that won't shut others down but will keep the spirit of the room safe:

- Maybe we could find a phrase or melody that's less expected?
- I don't know if that's in the language of the song.[2]
- Let's write that down![3]
- Let's stop writing and worship and listen!
- That sounds more like a hymn lyric … or a pop song. '
- Let me think about that.
- Maybe that's a bridge?
- I'm not sure that connects with me.
- Sing it for me!
- What are you hearing?
- I wonder if we can beat that.
- Do you think that is congregational?

Do you see a pattern here? Asking questions or seasoning your responses with grace is so helpful to other creatives. Questions help us express our openness; harsh opinions sound more closed.

Remembering that difference in a cowriting session will give more freedom.

It's important to remember that if we experience a negative spirit in the writing room, we ourselves can still carry a positive one that does not get crushed by it. It's also important to remember that you *will* have both good and bad cowriting experiences. I urge you to keep going if you have a bad experience. You will have good ones too. It may not have been cowriting that you didn't like; it may have been the spirit in the room.

You will grow in cowriting over time. My friend Leah Paschall said she came to a realization that the goal of the cowriting session is for the song to win, not any one person. I love that. We don't need to strive to get control of the room. It's no competition. It's building together. And in its most pure form, cowriting creates a dance of lyric and melody that we could never ever find on our own. It's worth it.

Take a moment to look up your favorite songs. Were they cowritten?

To hear more about cowriting, listen to the conversation Lani Crump and I had with professional songwriter Tony Wood (who has had thirty-one number-one songs on Christian radio!). You can find it in our resources at www.krissynordhoff.com/book.

Cowriting Exercise

Let's try this out so you can experience cowriting. Find a friend or two you'd like to write with. Plan a day, time, and place, whether online or in person. Set aside about four hours. When I go to a cowriting session, I usually pack my computer, computer cord, phone, phone cord, snacks (definitely chocolate), and a drink. Also, bring your three song ideas.

Get the Wi-Fi password and connect your computer. Open your tabs, as we discussed in chapter 8, "Song Mapping, Roots, and Resources."

Remember to take some time getting to know one another; then share your ideas and narrow them down to one. You can also use psalming to give you ideas. You can song map. Strengthen what you have with roots. But most of all, worship and have fun!

If you get a verse or a chorus, great! If you come back with a song, great! If all you accomplished was worship, great! Just enjoy the process.

10

Song Critiquing

There is no such thing as good writing; there is only good rewriting.
Harry Shaw, *Writing and Rewriting*

Rewriting—and the willingness to embrace it—is absolutely necessary for crafting great songs. Some of my favorite songs have been those that took months to complete. So much thought and heart were poured into them. Now, don't get me wrong; the Holy Spirit can drop a gem and change all that. But in general, songs require rewriting. Over time you begin to see it as just a part of the process.

I am often asked, "Would you critique one of my songs?" Getting your songs critiqued by others saves you time and can help periodically with finding direction. But I want to emphasize that it is *way* more important for you to learn how to do it yourself. (I remember having only one song critique ever before I became a staff songwriter.)

The more you are aware of the things we've learned and how to use them, the less rewriting you will need to do. The goal here is for most of the editing to happen in real time while the song is being written. If you can do that, you will save yourself and your cowriters a lot of time and frustration. Eventually, editing becomes second nature, and you'll do it without thinking. Now, I realize that starting out you will need to critique after you write until you begin to strengthen your rewriting muscles. That's OK for now. You will naturally make that transition when the time is right.

Through the previous chapters, we learned lots about qualities and devices that add strength to songs. Let's take just a moment to review these. They are important to compile because in doing so, we can create a checklist for you to review as you critique and edit your songs.

Song Critique Checklist

Top Ten Characteristics of Worship Songs

1. The songs are true and biblically accurate because song teaches theology.
2. Worship songs have community voice.
3. They have a simple, memorable melody and lyrics.
4. They stay close to an octave in range.
5. They often contain elements already familiar to the church.
6. They always include hope thematically.
7. They show a greater picture.
8. They can tell the story of the gospel.
9. They call us to respond in some way.
10. They can remind us of what's to come!

Song Mapping

- all ideas clearly support one central idea
- verses: reasons, feelings, explanations, lists, details

- chorus: big idea, title, the "Why?" "Where?" "Who?" or "What?" answer to the verses
- bridge: "Why else?" with a twist, gives a deeper meaning to the chorus
- prechorus: a connecting piece, adds smoothness either lyrically or musically between what is presented in the verses and the chorus

Lyrical Tools

- alliteration
- end rhyme
- internal rhyme
- near rhyme
- imagery
- simile
- personification
- metaphor
- hyperbole

Musical Tools

- prosody
- repetition
- meter
- drone

Impact Tools

- contrast
- space
- snowball
- suspense
- octave punch

Things to Watch For

- syllable emphasis
- syllable count
- inversion
- pronouns

To Begin Critiquing One of Your Songs

1. Print out the lyric sheet of a song or partial song you have written, and have the recording handy.
2. Print out the Song Critique Checklist. You can find it at www.krissynordhoff.com/book.
3. Play your song one section at a time while referencing the Song Critique Checklist, stopping as needed. As you do, be open to what you may find. Be willing to see discrepancies. Ask yourself questions such as these:
   - Is my song biblically true?
   - What other characteristics of worship songs does my song have?
   - Did I stay on track with my song map?
   - What type of rhyme did I use?
   - Did I include any imagery?
   - Can I see any other lyrical tools?
   - Did I use prosody in my song?
   - What other musical tools did I use?
   - Did I use the snowball technique?
   - What other impact tools did I use?

- Do all my syllables have the correct emphasis?
- Was I careful not to use inversion?
- Was I consistent with the use of pronouns?

A lot of questions, right? These are the things professional writers ask themselves about every song, most of the time subconsciously.

Unemotionally going over this checklist and checking for areas of your song that don't line up allow you to make improvements. Every time you make a change for the better, you learn and remember. The next time you come across a similar issue, you will correct it more quickly.

Another way to learn more is by listening to and studying other songs—songs you hear at church, on iTunes, or on Apple Music. Some of this you will have to learn by "feel." Some you will learn by dissecting the lyric or melody.

Remember, a big part of song critiquing is removing distractions such as inconsistent syllable counts, inconsistent pronouns, odd rhymes, and syllables with the wrong emphasis. Anything that stops worship and causes stumbling in any way needs to be pulled out of the song. Recently I was critiquing a worship song that had the word *mold* in it. It was meant in a shaping sort of way, but where it was placed made me picture fungus. Remove as many distractions as you can so that people can stay focused on worship!

Also, remember that context matters. I once heard a worship song from the UK that mentioned loving Jesus more than wine. That line works in the UK but could be misunderstood in some churches in the US. Keep culture in mind as you revise your songs.

Rewriting Exercise

I bet you can guess what I'm going to ask you to do! Pull out a song—or a piece of a song—that you would like to critique. Follow the directions on page 150, and walk through a section of the song at a time. Remember, the goal is to steward this song in the best way possible at this moment. Add strength and interest, but remove distractions. When you are finished, listen to the difference the rewriting made.

If the song you chose was cowritten, invite your cowriter or cowriters into the rewriting process in person, over Skype or FaceTime, or via email. If they can't join you, carry on with the rewriting and send them your new ideas for approval.

Sometimes melody changes are hardest. We get the old melody stuck in our heads and have a hard time moving on. But be willing to simply see what you're working on as a new song or a new piece of the song, and eventually you will have a breakthrough.

Pull in a cowriter if you get stuck. You may need his or her strength to finish the song in the best possible way.

Using the Song Critique Checklist and asking the right questions will definitely make your songs stronger. Over time, if you keep using this process, it will become ingrained in you and in your real-time writing, which is the goal!

Do I believe you should rewrite every song? Probably not. Especially if you're writing a lot of songs, this can get challenging because of the time involved. So how do you know which ones to focus on? I would say the ones you are passionate about. Make sure those are right. Chances are that if you are passionate about a song, someone else will be too.

11

The Songs in Your Blood

I'm done writing for: for practice, for projects, for churches, for others, for an upbeat slot, for a ballad slot. I want to write because: because I feel His love afresh, because I see new mercy, because I'm moved to worship, because I can't help it, because it's in my blood.

Krissy Nordhoff

Did you know there are songs literally inside you? Truly there are. According to modern science, our DNA can be charted and played musically. Each person has a unique song written into his or her DNA. How much more will science discover in the future about this correlation between the body and song?[1]

I gained a new appreciation and deeper understanding of the songs in me when I took a trip to Scotland with Ray and Denise Hughes. They led our group of eighteen, mostly songwriters, on a tour in late 2017. It's hard to put such a life-changing trip into words, but basically we traveled together for ten days, visiting spiritually significant places, hearing rich stories of history, and learning how these things affected the church and the world. We spent the last three days at Carberry Tower with our friends Jill and Andrew Mitchell, writing worship songs and worshipping together.

The very first day, we arrived in Edinburgh and ventured down the Royal Mile with Ray and Denise. I knew I had family lines that ran through Scotland, and I brought a little list of relatives' names that I carried in my pocket in case any of those names came up.

The first story Ray shared was about a man named James Guthrie. James was a Covenanter, a significant leader in a group that agreed to stand against religious oppression being mandated by the king. In fact, Guthrie was martyred for his beliefs in 1661 right there on the street. That place is still marked today in bricks on the street near the Mercat Cross. As I stood over it, I felt something in my spirit.

I looked down at my list. I had a James Guthrie in my line, but he was born forty years after this man died. I wondered about the space between.

That night, Ray sent us out in groups to pray over the city of Edinburgh. My roomie, Amber, agreed to join me back at the Mercat Cross. I felt as if I needed to sing "Your Great Name" out loud over the place where Guthrie was martyred. I wanted to continue proclaiming what he was stopped from proclaiming. So I stood there and sang alone. She videoed. We heard some defiant screams from someone on the street right when I sang the name of Jesus. We could feel the pull between light and dark that had been there for centuries.

The next day, we visited Greyfriars Kirk. Inside the church we saw an original copy of the covenant these Covenanters signed in 1638. In the graveyard, we visited the mass grave of one hundred Covenanters, including James Guthrie. On the gravestone itself, in bold, were the words *lamb*, *king*, *Jesus*, and *worthy*, among others. My friend Lisa noticed and said, "Krissy, what if that *is* your grandfather? Look at all the words from 'Your Great Name' on the gravestone."

Toward the end of our trip, in Stirling, Scotland, Ray mentioned there was a church built by James Guthrie that we could possibly go see the next day. I was still so curious about the possible connection. I thought I would try researching one more time that night and, with the help of European ancestry sites, found within three clicks that James Guthrie, the martyr, was my eleventh grandfather.

We had just enough time the next day to see the chapel. Denise, Lisa, Amber, and I all waited anxiously outside the door as Ray knocked. Ray had spoken at this church some years before, right after his first grandchild was born (a grandson named Guthrie). The woman who opened the door remembered Ray and Denise. As we stepped inside, I felt breathless. I got to sing at the front of the chapel while playing the grand piano. Tears welled up as I had a moment of realization: I had written a song straight from the bloodline of the Guthrie family.

The motto of the Guthrie family is "I stand for truth." Do you remember the reason I told you I wanted to write "Your Great Name"? It was to proclaim the truth about who Jesus is! Ray told me that James Guthrie spoke the truth in word, but the same truth flows through me and comes out in song.

We then went to the cemetery beside Stirling Castle. I picked up red poppies on the way and laid them at the feet of James Guthrie's memorial statue.

A year later, my friends and I were writing a song about the Covenanters. We pulled up the National Covenant to see exactly what these men had agreed to. To my surprise, they all swore by "the great name of the Lord our God."[2]

"Your Great Name" wasn't just my song. It was a song of my ancestors.

I told my sister years ago, "I feel like we have a spiritual heritage we know nothing about." This Guthrie story definitely seems like an answer to that wondering. Many times we don't know a lot about the generations that came long before us. Let me assure you there are many who are cheering you on right now in the "great cloud of witnesses" mentioned in Hebrews 12:1 (NIV). There are centuries-old prayers being answered and promises being fulfilled through you. You're part of a beautiful legacy … worthy of singing.

The Life of a Song

After my boys were born and I walked through Lyme disease, the doctors told me not to get pregnant again. I honestly couldn't imagine what my body would go through if I did, but I had this feeling deep down that we were missing somebody. A little girl.

As you know, the Lord healed me in an amazing way, but I still feared getting pregnant. We started researching adoption. We prayed. And then one night I had a "more real than real life" kind of dream. In my dream I gave birth to a baby. The doctor held the baby up and said, "Her name is Anthem."

I woke up and shared the dream with the boys and Eric. They all thought that was a weird name. I did too. A couple of months later, I flew out to visit my sister, who had moved to the Phoenix area. I didn't know until I got there that she was actually closer to a town called Anthem, Arizona. I was blown away driving down the highway, as every sign we passed continued to scream "Anthem!"

That year at Christmas, I kept hearing the word *anthem* in the carols. I also saw it many times as I was reading my Bible. One verse in 2 Chronicles in *The Message* says it three times (35:25).

Then a year and a half after I had that dream, I got pregnant. We were not trying to get pregnant, but we did. Immediately my blood pressure went sky high. My doctor told me I may need to consider terminating the pregnancy. We fired him and got a new doctor! We knew who this was, this girl of my dreams.

Around twenty weeks we all went in for the ultrasound together—Eric, the boys, and I. The baby looked completely healthy, despite some of my challenges along the way. We were thrilled when we found out it was a *girl*—it was her! We began texting friends and family. Not the usual "it's a boy" or "it's a girl" kind of messages. We texted, "IT'S ANTHEM!"

I visited the emergency room at least five times for high blood pressure during my pregnancy. The first time was at twenty weeks, and they told me I may have to be induced that night. But I wasn't afraid because I had already seen in my dream that she would be a full-grown, healthy girl. She was born at thirty-nine and a half weeks. It all happened just like in my dream.

We have loved every minute of watching Anthem grow. Eric, the boys, and I. We all know she's a miracle. But she's also a song. She carries melodies and lyrics everywhere she goes. I have a feeling one day you'll hear all about it.

She's the song that couldn't be stopped. The Lord Himself breathed life into her, and she will live the life that He—and no one else—determines.

The same is true of my other songs. And yours.

The Significance of Worship Songs

People often wonder what to do with the songs they've written. Sometimes I feel the same way. Some years I've written three hundred songs and thirty of them find a home (a typical percentage in our industry for a pro writer). But what about the other 270 that are sitting in the catalog from that year alone? Did it matter, all the hours it took to write them?

I was journaling one day, and I heard the Lord say, "Every song has spiritual significance."

Wow. It reminded me of when He said that when He hears my songs, He hears my voice. The songs matter to Him.

I once heard Andi Rozier from Vertical Worship share a powerful message about songwriting. He said our songs are like sailboats. We build them and put them in the water, and then the Holy Spirit is the wind that decides where they need to go.

We need to think about writing worship songs the way we think about praying. We don't stop praying when we don't get the answer we want. We trust God for the outcome.

Sometimes we can see that outcome, as in 2 Chronicles 20:22: "As they began to sing and praise, the LORD set ambushes against the men of Ammon and Moab and Mount Seir who were invading Judah, and they were defeated" (NIV). Song of praise … ambushes … victory. So amazing.

I would venture to say, though, that most of the time we don't see the outcome. We have to remember that so much happens in the "heavenly realms," as the Bible mentions in Ephesians (6:12 NIV). Just because we can't see doesn't mean there are not strongholds obliterated, fears bound, darkness defeated, curses broken, and wars for our hearts won when we sing to the Lord.

Whether we see or don't see, we need to trust the Lord for the outcome.

Don't let your heart get off balance in thinking your songs will be significant only when they reach a world-sized platform. That's a lie. There are so many other ways our songs can be significant to the kingdom. Let's look at a few.

The Five Purposes of Worship Songs

To Bless God Alone

"I will sing of your love and justice; to you, LORD, I will sing praise" (Ps. 101:1 NIV).

For example, "Revelation Song."[3]

Sometimes when I sit down at the piano and sing spontaneous worship to the Lord, it puts me in this place. I'm truly just worshipping Him for no other reason than to sing Him a song. Worship moves His heart in ways we may never know. Who knows how many angel armies have been sent out because of moments like these? Andi Rozier once questioned what God's favorite song was and wondered if God would one day answer, "Do you remember that song you sang for Me … this one at the piano, when it was just Me and you … the one no one ever heard? That was it."

To Bless God and Me Personally

"Worship the LORD your God, and his blessing will be on your food and water. I will take away sickness from among you" (Ex. 23:25 NIV).

For example, "Good, Good Father"[4] and "Reckless Love."[5]

Sometimes I worship the Lord through song and hear a message from Him as I sing. But hearing a message is not expected. Usually I experience tears and some kind of healing. God blesses me as I bless Him. My heart has been so encouraged in deep, deep ways by these moments.

To Bless Others in Their Relationship with God

"He put a new song in my mouth, a hymn of praise to our God. Many will see and fear the LORD and put their trust in him" (Ps. 40:3 NIV).

For example, "O Come to the Altar."[6]

I can't tell you how many songs for weddings, songs for people in need, songs for the sick, songs for celebrations, songs for funerals, and songs for new babies I've written—all reminders of the goodness of God. Will they ever get cut (put on an album)? Probably not. Did they bless someone? Yes. I've sung them over first breaths and last breaths and when no one had the words to speak. I believe these types of songs bless the church at large more than we will ever know on this earth.

To Praise God Corporately, to Bless God, and to Edify the Body

"Come, let us sing for joy to the LORD; let us shout aloud to the Rock of our salvation" (Ps. 95:1 NIV).

For example, "Jesus, We Love You."[7]

These are the songs individual church bodies need to hear. They speak the dialect a church understands, bringing hope, encouragement, and peace in ways that hit worship songs never could.

Sometimes they teach; sometimes they lead. It's always specific to what that particular body needs at the time. Many times these songs are for a specific season. They help carry the body through trials by reminding them where to focus their hearts. These songs also help churches express joy. They bring unity to the congregation.

To Worship God with the Global Church

"Shout for joy to the LORD, all the earth, burst into jubilant song with music" (Ps. 98:4 NIV).

For example, "Shout to the Lord"[8] and "How Great Is Our God."[9]

These are songs for the church at large. They reach across many denominations. When we gather in stadiums, these songs give us an avenue to praise the Lord all together. They bring unity to the church. As thousands of believers sing together, we get a greater picture of heaven and realize the gravity of praise.

Write from Your Heart

Friend, don't feel pressure to write things that aren't you. Don't be tempted to write about things you've never experienced. Don't strive to be trendy. Write from experience. Write from your most real self. Write from your heart. Write the songs in your blood.

Keep writing songs even when you don't get the outcome you wanted. I've never been successful at trying to write a song for the global church. But I've watched as what I thought was a song to bless God alone became a song for the whole church.

We pray, we write, and we trust God alone for what comes next. We write to give. To serve. We write because we have to. And if we are truly giving from an honest place, we don't expect to get anything back.

Keep your eyes on Jesus. He hears your every song. Every one is significant in ways we may never see. You build and create as you were meant to do. Let Him take care of the wind.

12

The Blessings

The LORD bless you and keep you; the LORD make
his face shine on you and be gracious to you.

Numbers 6:24–25 NIV

You were created with the gifts you have for this time and place. There is room for your gifts. Sometimes you may *feel* as if there is no room for your gifts. No room for your songs. It might look like Bethlehem ... *no room*. But let me tell you, God loves to find room where no one else does. He's the room maker.

When people offered no place for the Savior to be born, God made a barn holy. And while He could have shared the news of His Son first with great kings, He sent an angel to a few humble shepherds. And though there were no people announcing or celebrating Jesus' birth below, God's massive choir of angels did above (see Luke 2:4–14). He loves the unlikely.

So don't let anyone tell you there isn't room. It's the humble beginnings that give Him glory. Not just the calculated, not just the planned, not just the expected. He can use people like you and me.

I'm so honored that you chose to sit at the table with me. I hope you have been filled with fresh bread. I hope there are things from our conversations that you will carry both in your heart and in your songwriting as you go from here.

As we wrap up, I would like to bless you with the Songwriter's Prayer and the Songwriter's Commission. These are blessings from me to you. Feel free to come back and read them on days you need encouragement. They won't expire.

It is traditional in my church, at the end of the service, to hold out your hands for the blessing. So, if you'd like to do that now, you can. It's a simple way of demonstrating that your heart is ready to receive.

The Songwriter's Prayer

Lord, make ready the writers! Let them see You in detail and be left completely awestruck. Let them accurately write from hearts of wonder. Let the songs carry Your Spirit, changing hearts and lives with even one line. Let them write from the joy and freedom You give, all the while keeping in mind and upholding the truth. Then, Lord, use these messages, these songs, to have an impact not only on our generation but also on those to come. Above all else, may the songs be pure and fragrant offerings to You and bring only You glory. As we are blessed with songs, may You be the most blessed by hearing them.

The Songwriter's Commission

Now go ... and keep your heart in the birthplace of worship: the crossroads of honesty, love, discipline, and sacrifice.

Now go … and don't let the enemy trip you up with boulders; keep your path clear.

Now go … and don't forget who you are and what you're called to do.

Now go … and focus on your strengths and work to build the areas of weakness.

Now go … and sing aloud the ancient songs, letting the Holy Spirit teach you as you sing.

Now go … and be detailed in the process, and you will see great fruit.

Now go … and remember that true kingdom is built side by side.

Now go … and be flexible, teachable, and open to more growth.

Now go … and write the songs in your blood.

Now go … and trust the Holy Spirit to be your wind.

Now go … into all the earth. Into churches, hospitals, schools, and businesses. Into subways, planes, trains, and buses. Into villages, the countryside, towns, and cities.

Now go … into every nation, to every people, every tribe, and every tongue.

Now go … and tell of the good news. The forgiveness, the grace, the mercy, the joy. The comfort, the healing, the kindness, the peace through your song.

Now go … from today until He calls you home. Don't stop … just go!

Conclusion

What's Next?

If you'd like to learn about going deeper into the process of writing worship, here are the steps to follow:

READ IT → *WATCH IT* → *DO IT*

You've already read it (this book). Remember, you can always dive deeper into the resources related to the book at www.krissynordhoff .com/book.

Next, watch it; then do it. Here's how that looks, practically speaking:

Watch It

The Writing Worship Course. This is an introductory video course that demonstrates many of the concepts of this book. We explore two-way journaling, psalming, and song mapping. You will also have the opportunity to watch part of a live cowriting session. You can find this at www.krissynordhoff.com/course.

Do It

The Worship Songwriter Mentorship. This is an intensive nine-week multimedia online course. You'll have the opportunity to learn in a safe small group of twelve or fewer through weekly online calls, videos, songwriting assignments, and cowriting. Your small-group leader will be mentored by me personally. We'll take everything you've learned so far and put it into action in a community setting. Here's what's included in the mentorship:

- eight sessions with video teachings
- a downloadable PDF transcript of every video in each session
- downloadable PDF worksheets for each session, with fill-in-the-blanks to make it easy
- chord charts, plus audio and video links, for all the worship song examples
- an online small group committed to helping you finish, keeping you accountable, and helping you grow and ask questions
- an engaged, private online community where you can share songs, ask for song feedback, and connect with other songwriters for cowriting
- a printable certificate of completion at the end

Because of the small-group structure of the mentorship program, this is offered only seasonally throughout the year. You can find this at www.krissynordhoff.com/mentorship.

Live Events

Throughout the year I speak at many events, work with church worship teams, teach at conferences, and organize writing retreats. For more information about my schedule and any of my live events, visit www.krissynordhoff.com/events.

Worship Teams

Consider using this book as a resource for a group study with your worship team. For a free leader's guide, visit www.krissynordhoff.com /book.

Also, there are group rates available for both the Writing Worship Course and the Worship Songwriter Mentorship.

Promoting Your Music

You may be interested in having your songs published, recorded, or marketed. Although I don't consider myself an expert in this area, I do know many people who are. Please check out www.krissynordhoff .com/resources, where you will find my recommendations for pursuing and promoting these creative endeavors.

Staying Connected

To hear my latest songs on Spotify, check out my playlist called "Krissy Nordhoff Songs" or go to www.krissynordhoff.com/spotify.

To hear my latest songs on Apple Music, search for "Krissy Nordhoff Songs" or go to www.krissynordhoff.com/applemusic.

Instagram: @krissy_nordhoff
Facebook: Krissy Nordhoff Music
Website: www.krissynordhoff.co

Notes

Chapter 1

1. Amy Grant, vocalist, "El Shaddai," by Michael Card and John Thompson, track 7 on *Age to Age*, Myrrh Records, 1982.

2. "Take My Life, and Let It Be," by Frances R. Havergal, 1874, public domain.

3. Natalie Grant, vocalist, "Your Great Name," by Krissy Nordhoff and Michael Neale, tracks 8 and 12 on *Love Revolution*, Curb Records, 2010.

4. "Alcatraz," written by Krissy Nordhoff, TwoNords Music. This song was never recorded.

Chapter 2

1. Upper Room Music, featuring Elyssa Smith, "Surrounded (Fight My Battles)," by Elyssa Smith, track 5 on *Moments EP*, UpperRoom/The Fuel Music, 2018.

2. John Calvin, *The Epistles of Paul the Apostle to the Galatians, Ephesians, Philippians, and Colossians*, Calvin's Commentaries (Grand Rapids, MI: Eerdmans, 1965), 134.

3. "Wisdom and Revelation by the Spirit," Ligonier Ministries, accessed October 30, 2019, www.ligonier.org/learn/devotionals/wisdom-and-revelation-spirit/.

4. Mandisa, vocalist, "Back to Life," by Michael Farren, Krissy Nordhoff, and James Galbraith, track 18 on *Out of the Dark*, deluxe ed., Sparrow Records, 2017. This is quoted according to Krissy's original writing, which had "resentment" instead of "shame."

5. Cross Point Music, featuring Zach Kale, "Watch What He Will Do," by Mike Grayson, Zach Kale, and Krissy Nordhoff, track 2 on *Cross Point Music EP*, Cross Point Music, 2019.

6. Anthony Evans, vocalist, "Fighting for Us," by Michael Farren and Krissy Nordhoff, track 4 on *Altared*, Sherman James Productions, 2019.

7. "What Does Ephesians 5:19 Mean?," BibleRef.com, accessed September 4, 2019, www.bibleref.com/Ephesians/5/Ephesians-5-19.html.

Chapter 3

1. Kristyn Getty, vocalist, "In Christ Alone," by Keith Getty and Stuart Townend, track 4 on *In Christ Alone*, Getty Music Label, 2006.

2. Bryan Torwalt and Katie Torwalt, vocalists, "Holy Spirit," by Bryan Torwalt and Katie Torwalt, track 2 on *Here on Earth*, Jesus Culture Music, 2011.

3. Housefires, "Good, Good Father," by Anthony Brown and Pat Barrett, track 7 on *Housefires II*, Housefires, 2014.

4. Bethel Music, featuring Kalley Heiligenthal, "Ever Be," by Kalley Heiligenthal et al., track 2 on *We Will Not Be Shaken (Live)*, Bethel Music, 2015.

5. Chris Tomlin, vocalist, "Amazing Grace (My Chains Are Gone)," by John Newton, Chris Tomlin, and Louie Giglio, track 11 on *See the Morning*, sixstepsrecords/Sparrow Records, 2006.

6. Matt Redman, vocalist, "Blessed Be Your Name," by Matt Redman and Beth Redman, track 2 on *Where Angels Fear to Tread*, Worship Together, 2002.

7. Chris Tomlin, vocalist, "How Great Is Our God," by Chris Tomlin, Jesse Reeves, and Ed Cash, track 3 on *Arriving*, sixstepsrecords/Sparrow Records, 2004.

8. Stuart Townend, vocalist, "How Deep the Father's Love," by Stuart Townend, track 9 on *Say the Word*, Integrity Music, 1989.

9. Hillsong Worship, "Forever Reign," by Jason Ingram and Reuben Morgan, track 3 on *A Beautiful Exchange (Live)*, Hillsong Church, 2010.

10. Kari Jobe, vocalist, "Revelation Song," by Jennie Lee Riddle, track 11 on *Kari Jobe*, Gateway Music, 2010.

11. This is the title of one of his books: Eugene H. Peterson, *A Long Obedience in the Same Direction: Discipleship in an Instant Society* (Downers Grove, IL: InterVarsity, 1980).

12. Smith Wigglesworth, quoted in Jesse Carey, "13 Smith Wigglesworth Quotes That Will Challenge Your Faith," *Relevant Magazine*, June 8, 2015, https://relevantmagazine.com/god/13-smith-wigglesworth-quotes-will-challenge-your-faith.

13. "It Is Well with My Soul: 1873," in Robert J. Morgan, *Then Sings My Soul: 150 Christmas, Easter, and All-Time Favorite Hymn Stories* (Nashville: Thomas Nelson, 2010), 203.

14. "Amazing Grace: 1779," in Morgan, *Then Sings My Soul*, 163.

15. Mike Miller, "The Painful True Story behind MercyMe Singer Bart Millard's Hit Faith-Based Movie," *People*, March 29, 2018, https://people.com/movies/bart-millard-faith-based-movie-true-story.

16. Natalie Grant, vocalist, "Your Great Name," by Krissy Nordhoff and Michael Neale, tracks 8 and 12 on *Love Revolution*, Curb Records, 2010.

Chapter 4

1. Daniel Doss, vocalist, "You Are the Bread," written by Daniel Doss and Krissy Nordhoff, video, 4:13, August 16, 2018, https://youtube.com/watch?v=_Uf97jolzKs.

2. Mark Batterson, *Draw the Circle: The 40 Day Prayer Challenge* (Grand Rapids, MI: Zondervan, 2012), 149.

Chapter 5

1. Dictionary.com, s.v. "identity," accessed September 9, 2019, www.dictionary.com/browse/identity.

2. Dr. Christopher Magovern, "10 Things You May Not Know about Your Heart," *ABC News*, February 14, 2012, https://abcnews.go.com/blogs/health/2012/02/14/10-things-you-may-not-know-about-your-heart.

Chapter 7

1. *Merriam-Webster*, s.v. "acrostic," accessed September 10, 2019, www.merriam-webster.com/dictionary/acrostic.

2. Stephen Broyles, "Praising the Law through the Alphabet: Reading Psalm 119 over the Author's Shoulder," Andreas Center, last modified November 20, 2009, www.andreascenter.org/Articles/Psalm%20119.htm.

Chapter 8

1. Corey Voss, featuring Krissy Nordhoff, "Canyons," by Corey Voss and Krissy Nordhoff, track 7 on *Songs of Heaven and Earth (Live)*, Integrity Music, 2018.

2. Mandisa, vocalist, "Back to Life," by Michael Farren, Krissy Nordhoff, and James Galbraith, track 18 on *Out of the Dark*, deluxe ed., Sparrow Records, 2017. This is quoted according to Krissy's original writing, which had "resentment" instead of "shame."

3. Hillsong UNITED, "Oceans (Where Feet May Fail)," by Joel Houston, Matt Crocker, and Salomon Ligthelm, track 4 on *Zion*, Hillsong Church, 2013.

4. "Amazing Grace," by John Newton, 1779, public domain.

5. Kari Jobe, vocalist, "Revelation Song," by Jennie Lee Riddle, track 11 on *Kari Jobe*, Gateway Music, 2010.

6. Anthony Evans, vocalist, "Fighting for Us," by Michael Farren and Krissy Nordhoff, track 4 on *Altared*, Sherman James Productions, 2019.

7. Bryan Torwalt and Katie Torwalt, vocalists, "Holy Spirit," by Bryan Torwalt and Katie Torwalt, track 2 on *Here on Earth*, Jesus Culture Music, 2011.

8. Michael W. Smith, vocalist, "Above All," by Lenny LeBlanc and Paul Baloche, track 13 on *Worship*, Reunion Records, 2001.

9. Hillsong UNITED, "So Will I (100 Billion X)," by Joel Houston, Michael Fatkin, and Benjamin Hastings, track 4 on *Wonder*, Hillsong Church, under exclusive license to Capitol CMG Label Group/Sparrow Records, 2017.

10. Jesus Culture, featuring Kim Walker-Smith, "How He Loves (Live)," by John Mark McMillan, track 8 on *This Is Jesus Culture (Live)*, Jesus Culture Music, under exclusive license to Sparrow Records, 2015.

11. Cory Asbury, vocalist, "Reckless Love," by Caleb Culver, Cory Asbury, and Ran Jackson, track 1 on *Reckless Love*, Bethel Music, 2018.

12. Voss, featuring Nordhoff, "Canyons," by Voss and Nordhoff.

13. Housefires, "Good, Good Father," by Anthony Brown and Pat Barrett, track 7 on *Housefires II*, Housefires, 2014.

14. Chris Tomlin, vocalist, "How Great Is Our God," by Chris Tomlin, Jesse Reeves, and Ed Cash, track 3 on *Arriving*, sixstepsrecords/Sparrow Records, 2004.

15. Kristyn Getty, vocalist, "In Christ Alone," by Keith Getty and Stuart Townend, track 4 on *In Christ Alone*, Getty Music Label, 2006.

16. Steffany Gretzinger, vocalist, "Pieces (Live)," by Amanda Lindsey Cook and Steffany Gretzinger, track 6 on *Have It All (Live)*, Bethel Music, 2016.

17. Jonathan David Helser and Melissa Helser, vocalists, "No Longer Slaves (Live)," by Jonathan David Helser, Brian Johnson, and Joel Case, track 4 on *We Will Not Be Shaken (Live)*, Bethel Music, 2015.

18. Steffany Gretzinger and Jeremy Riddle, vocalists, "King of My Heart (Live)," by John Mark McMillan and Sarah McMillan, track 6 on *Starlight (Live)*, Bethel Music, 2017.

19. Lacey Sturm, vocalist, "Mercy Tree," by Krissy Nordhoff and Michael Neale, track 11 on *My Hope: Songs Inspired by the Message and Mission of Billy Graham*, Sparrow Records, 2013.

20. Hillsong UNITED, "Lead Me to the Cross," by Brooke Fraser, track 6 on *All of the Above*, Hillsong Church, 2007.

21. Matt Maher, vocalist, "Lord, I Need You," by Jesse Reeves et al., track 4 on *All the People Said Amen (Live)*, Provident Label Group, 2013.

Chapter 9

1. Travis Cottrell, vocalist, "His Name Is Jesus," by Travis Cottrell, Krissy Nordhoff, and Ben Cantelon, track 2 on *Heaven's Hope EP*, Capitol Christian Music Group, 2018.

2. Thanks to Tony Wood.

3. Thanks to Paul Baloche.

Chapter 11

1. Marina Jones, "Is Music in Our DNA?," Futurism.com, February 13, 2014, https://futurism.com/is-music-in-our-dna.

2. Wikisource, s.v. "National Covenant of the Church of Scotland," last modified June 9, 2012, https://en.wikisource.org/wiki/National_Covenant_of_the_Church_of_Scotland.

3. Kari Jobe, vocalist, "Revelation Song," by Jennie Lee Riddle, track 11 on *Kari Jobe*, Gateway Music, 2010.

4. Housefires, "Good, Good Father," by Anthony Brown and Pat Barrett, track 7 on *Housefires II*, Housefires, 2014.

5. Cory Asbury, vocalist, "Reckless Love," by Caleb Culver, Cory Asbury, and Ran Jackson, track 1 on *Reckless Love*, Bethel Music, 2018.

6. Elevation Worship, "O Come to the Altar," by Chris Brown et al., track 4 on *Here as in Heaven (Live)*, Elevation Worship, 2016.

7. Hannah McClure, vocalist, "Jesus, We Love You (Live)," by Paul McClure, Hannah McClure, and Kalley Heiligenthal, track 3 on *We Will Not Be Shaken (Live)*, Bethel Music, 2015.

8. Darlene Zschech, vocalist, "Shout to the Lord," by Darlene Zschech, track 12 on *Shout to the Lord*, Integrity Music, 1996.

9. Chris Tomlin, vocalist, "How Great Is Our God," by Chris Tomlin, Jesse Reeves, and Ed Cash, track 3 on *Arriving*, sixstepsrecords/Sparrow Records, 2004.

About the Author

Krissy Nordhoff is a professional songwriter, cofounder of the Brave Worship community, and creator of the Worship Songwriter Mentorship. A Michigan native, Krissy grew up in a Christian home, sharing a love of church music with her family. She attended Anderson University, studied songwriting with the legendary Gloria Gaither, and later taught piano and performed as an indie artist.

Realizing that her dreams were shifting away from travel and performing as she and her husband, Eric, welcomed children, Krissy began to focus on songwriting. She poured her own tears and triumphs into songs birthed out of an ever-deepening relationship with God through each season of life. Along the way, she garnered three Dove Award nominations for her efforts and won a Dove Award for Worship Song of the Year for the beloved anthem "Your Great Name," inspired by her own health battle and God's healing. Her songs have been recorded by a variety of artists, including Natalie Grant, Jenn Johnson (Bethel Music), Tauren Wells, Mandisa, Darlene Zschech, David and Nicole Binion, Travis Cottrell, Corey Voss, Dustin Smith, Anthony Evans, Phillips, Craig and Dean, and many others. She has also written songs with worship teams, including Life.Church Worship, Cross Point Music, and Prestonwood Worship.

Passionate about training and encouraging the next generation of worship songwriters, Krissy now mentors and teaches and creates helpful resources, including informative podcasts and a "Songwriter Personality Test."

Krissy, Eric, and their three children live in Thompson's Station, Tennessee, near Nashville. For more information, visit www .krissynordhoff.com or www.braveworship.com.